The Dr. Gourmet Low Sodium Diet

Dr. Gourmet

Timothy S. Harlan, M.D.
and Morgan Ladd Harlan

The Dr. Gourmet Low Sodium Diet

Table of Contents

Introduction

You have likely purchased this book because your doctor has told you to follow a low sodium diet. This may seem like a big pain, and you might not be convinced that it is really necessary.

After reading this book, I believe you will find that a low sodium diet does not have to be a bother and can actually be not only easy but delicious as well. You'll understand how eating less salt can have a tremendous impact on your health, including helping to control your blood pressure, reduce the risk of stroke and improve your overall health. In the first part of the book, I'll share with you what we've learned about eating less sodium from all of the great research that's been done on sodium and health.

The second part of the book is a 6 week plan including meal plans, recipes and shopping lists. It's designed to serve two people, both eating 1,500 calories per day, but you can scale it up or down as needed.

In addition to this book there are extensive free resources available to you online at DrGourmet.com. You will find additional low-sodium recipes as well as an interactive meal planner that will help you continue creating weekly menus complete with shopping lists.

Eat well, eat healthy, enjoy life!

Timothy S. Harlan, M.D.
Dr. Gourmet

Low Sodium Quick-Start Guide

Here are a few steps that you can take right away to help reduce the sodium in your diet:

Step One: Take the processed food out of your life.

If you want Mac and Cheese, make Mac and Cheese. Cooking your own fresh food from scratch takes a little more time, but it tastes so much better and it's so much better for you. If you're used to frozen or packaged meals, snagging fast food for dinner or eating on the run, start slowly by making just two meals per week at home. Beyond the low sodium meals in this book there are hundreds more available to you on the DrGourmet. com Web site.

Step Two: Read food labels.

When you do eat packaged or processed foods, pay attention to the added salt. The sodium content is the one item on the Nutrition Facts label that isn't confusing. You can simply look at the number of milligrams on the label and choose items that are lower in salt. Simply eat less sodium and you'll likely prolong your life.

Step Three: Plan.

One main focus of this book is to help you understand the importance of planning. By creating weekly menus for yourself you are able to control what you eat. So many of us are simply reactive and decide what to eat a few minutes before lunch or dinner. Being proactive about what you eat and your health puts you in control of your health.

Step Four: Measure.

I see diet plans all the time that say you don't have to measure anything. This is simply not true. You do need to have some idea of what you are eating and this includes calories as well as sodium. By measuring and weighing your food, you will have an understanding of how well you are following your plan.

Always keep in mind that that the government's guideline of 2,400 mg sodium per day is about 1 teaspoon salt. (Your doctor may have given you a lower target.) Measure your salt carefully when you cook. It's easy and a simple step to being healthier.

10 Quick Tips for Eating Healthier

I have a list of quick tips that I use with patients when they ask about eating healthy. Often this is simply for people who are otherwise healthy and want to avoid the creeping weight gain that many people experience. It is also an easy place to start for those who want to lose weight.

1. Take half of your restaurant meal home with you. Because the portions in restaurants are so large, and you likely need only half of what you have been served, put the other half into the doggie bag. Hmm... that leads us to number two:

2. When you eat out, ask for a doggie bag right away. Order whatever you wish, but again, take half home with you. By putting what you are not going to eat in a doggie bag first, then you can eat everything that remains on the plate. And that leads us to number three:

3. Make your lunch the night before (or eat the leftover from your doggie bag). When you are cooking dinner, plan to use the extra rather than eating everything you've made. For instance, you can double a recipe that makes two servings and have four 1/2 servings for the next two day's lunches for yourself and your family. You will save time because not only is fast food not any good for you, it's not really all that fast any more.

And eating lunch out is expensive. If you spend $6.00 on lunch at the fast food joint (instead of the $1.00 or so making your own) that's $25.00 per week. You'll save $1,250.00 per year on lunch alone! That's enough for your gym membership with money left over for a trip to the beach and a week of R&R.

4. Embrace food. Ask yourself every day, "What's for dinner tonight?" Think about what you really want to eat rather than eating whatever is in the house. Find a simple recipe, make a shopping list, and get the ingredients. Consider the meal that you are going to cook and make sure that is something that you love.

After you have the hang of this, begin planning further in advance. Go grocery shopping for the week on Saturday and purchase the ingredients that you need to make your favorite recipes during the week (see Number 3).

5. Always have snacks on hand that you like to eat. The best things to snack on are fresh fruit and raw or roasted nuts. Plus, if you have something in the house that you can eat as much of as you want, you won't snack on what you were planning to use for dinner.

I have patients who say all the time, "I don't like fruit," or "There aren't any vegetables that I like." When I begin making a list for them of different fruits they're amazed how many they not only like, but love. Keep fruits that are easy to cut up and eat, like apples, pears and melons.

6. Read everything that you can. Read recipes in magazines and online. Look at the ingredients and then check the nutrition facts to see how many calories are in that meal. Don't make a dish if there's no nutrition information available with the recipe.

Look at every package of food or ingredient that you purchase and read the Nutrition Facts label. Over time you will learn what is in the food you are eating.

7. It's not a diet. Make changes in how and what you eat (see Number 4 about embracing food).

By trying silly fad diets over and over, most people just end up not liking what they eat. There have been dozens of research studies to show that this sort of dieting doesn't work.

Don't diet - eat great food.

8. A little chocolate goes a long way (and so does an apple). In a recent study women were surveyed after snacking on chocolate, an apple or nothing. Both the chocolate and the apple helped reduce huger and elevated mood. While the effects of the chocolate lasted longer than the apple, some did feel guilt when eating the chocolate.

Planning to have snacks when you want them is an important part of eating healthy. Choose great quality chocolate and have it occasionally - and at other times eat the apple. It's clear that both are satisfying. The key is to eat small snacks and to eat them when you feel good.

9. Eat nuts. Like apples, nuts make fantastic snacks. Many studies have shown that snacking on nuts is good for your cholesterol and other blood markers associated with heart disease. The majority of the research shows that when you eat nuts in place of other snacks, you won't gain weight and you'll be very satisfied.

10. Eat breakfast. Simple as that. There's great research that shows that eating a healthy breakfast with a complex carbohydrate like whole wheat bread or whole grain cereal, along with a protein like an egg or milk, helps you to lose weight and maintain what you have lost.

Add one of these tips to your life each week and ten weeks later you'll be eating healthier without even having to think about it.

Reducing Sodium Reduces Blood Pressure

Medicine is not like math.

Remember back in Algebra class where if A = B and B = C, then A = C? One of the reasons that we do research in as large a group of people as we can is because not all people's bodies react the same way to certain things. More people in a study is better because it's easier to see how most people will react.

This is why, as my wife is fond of saying, "The plural of anecdote is not data." Which is to say, one person's experience (an anecdote, or personal story) can not be said to be proof that something is true for everyone. If, out of 1,000 people (for example), the vast majority of people are having a certain reaction, however... that starts to look like proof (and even then more research may be needed).

You've probably been hearing for a long time now that reducing sodium intake will reduce your blood pressure, and that will lead to a lower risk of stroke, heart disease, and ultimately, death. While this is considered obvious to doctors because it's basic biochemistry, it's important to remember that sometimes medicine doesn't work as straightforwardly as all that. So where is the proof? Years ago there hadn't been many studies that demonstrated that a lower sodium diet would actually translate directly to a lower blood pressure. Fortunately, back in 1997 the *American Journal of Clinical Nutrition* published a study that pooled the results of thirty-two smaller studies that looked at the connection between salt in the diet and blood pressure.[1] Essentially they asked that basic question: "Does reducing sodium intake reduce blood pressure?"

The studies they included in their pooled results had to meet certain criteria, including participants being randomly assigned to the test group; blood pressure measurements of both systolic and diastolic measures (the top and bottom numbers in your blood pressure measurement); not using blood pressure medications for some participants and not others; objective reporting of sodium intake (as opposed to food records, which might not be accurate); adult participants; and, finally, when the participants reduced their sodium intake, that intake had to be to levels that were actually reasonable to achieve for people living in the real world.

That's a pretty tight set of criteria and led to a total of a little over 2,600 participants. Those participants who had high blood pressure at the start of the studies reduced their sodium intake by an average of almost 1800 milligrams per day. That might sound like a lot, but the average intake of salt for men in the United States is up to 10,000 milligrams. That means they were reducing their sodium intake by only 18%! Those folks with high blood pressure reduced their systolic blood pressures (the top number) by almost 5 points, and their diastolic blood pressure (the bottom number) by 2.5 points. That's something your doctor would consider significant.

Similarly, those whose blood pressure was normal at the start of their studies reduced their salt intake by about the same amount, and also saw their blood pressures reduced by meaningful amounts: a little over 2 points for systolic and about 1.5 points for diastolic. Is this an amount that matters? Definitely: a drop of just 3 points in our country's average systolic blood pressure means 11% fewer strokes, 7% fewer incidents of heart disease (including heart attack), and 5% fewer deaths from all causes.

Sodium and Stroke

We know that high levels of sodium in the diet are linked to high blood pressure and thus to the risk of stroke, but until recently few studies have attempted to link sodium and stroke more directly.

In a well-designed study published in the journal *Stroke*,[2] researchers at the University of Miami and Columbia University in New York City collaborated to use information gathered through a multiethnic study of diet and stroke based in Northern Manhattan. The over 2,600 participants in the researchers' analysis were between 50 and 80 years of age and had not previously experienced a stroke at the start of the ten-year study. Over half of the participants (53%) were Hispanic, while 21% were white and 24% black.

At the start of the study the participants answered a detailed dietary questionnaire to help determine their daily sodium intake. Every year thereafter the participants were recontacted to discuss their current health, including any hospitalizations, medication changes, or changes in stroke risk factors (such as smoking).

Interestingly, only 12% of the participants were meeting the most stringent recommendation of less than 1,500 milligrams of sodium per day. Slightly more than one third of the participants were under the USDA recommendation of less than 2,400 milligrams per day, while 21% were consuming over 4,000 milligrams of sodium per day.

The researchers then compared the sodium intake of those who experienced stroke of any kind or a heart attack with those who did not. They found that compared to those meeting the 1,500 mg recommendation, those who were consuming over 4,000 milligrams of sodium per day were more than 2 and a half times more likely to have a stroke. In fact, every increase of sodium intake of 500 milligrams per day increased the risk of stroke by 17%: an intake of 2,500 milligrams per day meant a 34% increase in risk; 3,000 milligrams per day was a 51% increase in risk, and so on.

While the USDA recommends 2,400 mg per day for most Americans, it further recommends that those over 50, black, or suffering from diabetes, high blood pressure or kidney disease limit their intake to 1,500 mg per day. This study certainly supports the American Heart Association's recommendation that all Americans reduce their intake to under 1,500mg day.

Sodium and Your Heart

One of the earliest signs of impending heart disease is a decline in the ability of very small coronary arteries to relax (or not). The measurement of this ability of these blood vessels to relax is known as Coronary Flow Reserve (CFR), and a low measurement is considered a poor score.

By now you know that a diet high in sodium can affect your overall blood pressure, which can lead to heart attack and stroke. Researchers at Emory University in Atlanta; University of Washington in Seattle, Washington; and the US Department of Veterans' Affairs collaborated to find out if sodium intake had an effect on CFR.[3]

They made use of data collected from the Emory Twins Heart Study, which was made up of members of the Vietnam Era Twin Registry. This is a group of male twins, raised in the same family, who served in the US military between 1964 and 1975. Research on twins is especially valuable because of their genetic similarity, which in this case allows researchers to better understand the impact of individual diet having to take into account variation between non-twin individuals. In short, the impact of diet is easier to see because the researchers can compare two different diets in what is genetically the same person.

As part of the study, researchers performed PET scans on the hearts of the participants and were able to compute their CFR. A detailed dietary questionnaire allowed them to assess the participants' sodium intake.

After also taking into account such variables as blood pressure, cholesterol scores, smoking status and physical activity, the researchers found that a poor CFR score was strongly related to higher sodium intake. In fact, for every additional 1000 milligrams of sodium consumed per day, a participant's CFR decreased by 10%. Those in the two highest levels of sodium intake (out of 5 levels) all had CFR scores in the abnormal range - which is believed to be linked to a greater risk of heart attack and death from heart disease.

It is becoming clearer that higher sodium intake affects your heart's function at a very basic level - much more basic than simple blood pressure.

The Taste of Salt

The developed world eats a tremendous amount of sodium in their diet. The average person consumes over 6,000 milligrams (mg) of sodium every day (and recent estimates put that maybe as high as 10,000 milligrams per day). That 6,000 milligrams works out to about 2 1/2 teaspoons of salt, which is about 2 1/2 times the currently recommended amount of 2,400 mg per day. This is true not only in the U.S., but the United Kingdom has also had a longstanding campaign aimed at convincing people to reduce the amount of salt they consume. Most Asian diets are high in sodium as well, with almost every sauce, from soy sauce to fish sauce to hoisin, having added salt.

A report by the Council on Science and Public Health[4] estimates that such a lowering of salt intake might save

150,000 lives each year - that's a lot of your friends, family, and coworkers. That makes reducing salt intake for the population as a whole into a big issue for policy makers. The challenge is that there is so much added salt in the processed foods that Americans eat.

For many people, however, the 2,400 mg per day recommendation is still too much salt. We know from the research that cutting sodium even further, to 1,500 mg per day, can have a profound effect on people's health, including preventing and treating high blood pressure and congestive heart failure. This book will help you reach those goals of 2,000 mg or lower.

If you are used to eating a lot of salt, there is great research to show that your tastebuds can learn to do without all that sodium. One study placed a group of people on a sodium restricted diet for five months.[5] Their response to the saltiness of salt in solutions, soups and crackers was measured before the study and while they were following the diet. The same measurements were made in a control group that didn't change their diet. In the group that lowered their salt intake, the perceived intensity of salt in crackers increased over the five month period. Because they were used to eating less salt on a daily basis, the same crackers seemed saltier!

Further, the amount of salt needed to make the test foods taste their best fell in the study group but not in the control group. In effect, the more you saturate your taste buds, the more you can't taste how salty something is. If you are used to salty foods, over time you will grow accustomed to less salt when you consume less sodium.

In a particularly interesting study, researchers in The Netherlands looked at people's responses to reduced sodium levels in bread.[6] They recruited 116 men and women from the staff and students of Wageningen University, where the researchers were based, and were assigned to one of three groups. On weekdays for four weeks, the participants ate a buffet breakfast at the university's Restaurant of the Future. Each group had the same breakfast buffet, which offered bread and an array of savory or sweet toppings or fillings for the bread, along with corn flakes, various fruits, orange juice, coffee and tea.

The difference between the three groups was the bread. The control group received the same type of bread throughout the four weeks of the study. For the second group, the sodium content of the bread was reduced, week by week. Week 1 was the standard bread, then for week 2 the sodium content was reduced by 31%. For week 3 the sodium content was reduced further, to just 52%, and finally in week 4 the sodium content was reduced by 67% - so it contained just one-third of the sodium in the standard bread. The third group also received bread with the same reductions in sodium, but their bread included potassium chloride, a commonly-used salt substitute.

The researchers monitored the breakfast choices of all of the participants and were able to measure each person's caloric intake as well as how much sodium was in their breakfast meal. They found that even though the bread was less salty, the participants did not appear to choose saltier toppings to make up for the reduction in sodium, indicating that they did not notice that the bread was less salty. At the close of the study, all of the participants were asked to taste each of the breads used in the study and rate them in terms of pleasantness, saltiness, tenderness and whether the bread had an "off-flavor."

As you might expect, those in the control group (who had received regular bread all along) rated the reduced-sodium breads lower on the saltiness scale, while those who had received the reduced-sodium breads rated all of the breads higher on the saltiness scale. It appears that their taste buds had become accustomed to the lower levels of salt in their bread. Those who received bread with the salt substitute rated saltiness for all of the breads in between the ratings from the other two groups.

The problem with salt substitutes like potassium chloride, however, is that you can only use so much of before it starts to give that product a bitter, metallic flavor.

Researchers with Unilever, one of the world's largest food companies, have been looking at different ways they might reduce the sodium content in foods without compromising flavor. The flavor effects of reducing sodium in a food, they noted, isn't limited to reducing the food's perceived saltiness: it also affects other components of flavor as well as reducing the food's overall flavor intensity. Would other ways of boosting flavor help compensate for lower sodium?

As flavor researchers they were aware that the sense of smell has a strong interaction with and influence on the sense of taste. (Just try eating with your nose plugged and you'll see how strong that influence can be.) In fact, research has been done that shows that cheese tastes less salty if the taster uses nose clips during tasting.

They decided to test aroma enhancements on chicken and beef broth - both of which depend quite a bit on the salt they contain for fullest flavor.[7] Ten men and women tasted each of the following broths and rated them on salt intensity and overall intensity of flavor:

> Regular, full-sodium-level broth;
> Broth with 30% less sodium;
> Broth with 30% less sodium and added beef or chicken flavor (and therefore scent); and
> Broth with 30% less sodium, added beef or chicken flavor, and potassium chloride as a salt replacement

They found that the broth with less sodium and added flavoring was perceived to be almost as salty as the original, while the broth with less sodium, added flavoring and the salt replacement was considered to be almost indistinguishable from the original.

To go even further, the researchers gave the chicken broth to a trained panel of tasters - people who are able to discern the smallest differences in flavor and use a standardized set of terms to describe the flavors accurately. The tasters agreed that the reduced-sodium chicken broth was less "salty" and "umami" and had a lower "full-ness" of flavor than the original, full-sodium broth - as you might expect, since salt is used as a flavor enhancer. Adding only the salt replacement to the reduced-sodium chicken broth did not restore the "salty," "umami," and "fullness" scores and added a noticeable metallic flavor (remember, these are trained tasters). However, adding the extra chicken flavoring to a slightly lower level of salt replacement meant that the panel could only perceive a difference between it and the full-sodium original when they directly compared the two.

This is proof that sodium can be reduced without compromising flavor. It's encouraging to know that companies like Unilever are pursuing this kind of research. Many companies, such as Lean Cuisine, are already doing this by using potassium chloride in place of some of the sodium in their food, although this doesn't mean that you should take this as permission to eat convenience foods.

Blood Pressure, Salt, and Potassium

We know that diets low in sodium help to lower blood pressure. What you may not know is that diets that are high in potassium, such as vegetarian diets and those high in fruits in vegetables, can also help reduce blood pressure.

Researchers in Australia noted that the Australian intake of fruits and vegetables tends to be a good 50% higher than the American diet - meaning that it's much higher in potassium. Previous research showed that those Australians with mild high blood pressure benefitted from a diet low in sodium - would those who did not have high blood pressure also benefit from a low-sodium diet, given that their typical diet is high in potassium already?

To find out, the researchers recruited 92 men and women with normal or slightly elevated blood pressures to participate in a dietary study.[8] The participants were all taught to follow a low-sodium, high-potassium diet for 8 weeks, while their blood pressures were monitored regularly. The goal of the diet was to cut their usual sodium intake by more than half, and to help reach that goal the researchers provided the participants with salt-free bread, salt-free margarine, and other low-sodium ingredients. (Note that they were not instructed to use salt substitutes containing potassium.) The participants were instructed to avoid processed foods and higher-sodium snack foods and to replace their snack foods with vegetables, fruits, and nuts - all high in potassium.

For the first four weeks of the study, half of the participants received sodium supplements intended to return the sodium levels of their diet to the higher levels found in a typical Australian's diet. The other half of the participants received a placebo. For the second four weeks, the two groups switched: instead of salt tablets, the first group received the placebos, while the second group received the salt tablets. This allowed the researchers to compare the effects of a high-sodium diet with high potassium levels with the effects of a low-sodium diet with high potassium levels.

They found that even those whose diets were already high in potassium would indeed benefit from a reduced-sodium diet: those participants who started the study with normal blood pressures saw their systolic blood pressure (the top number) reduced by about 2.5 points when they followed the high-potassium, low-sodium diet (the placebo phase). Even more importantly, when the subjects were following the low-sodium, high-potassium diet and were receiving the salt tablets, their blood pressures were still lower than when they started the study - although not as low as when they received the placebos.

By no means should you take this as a directive to go out and take a potassium supplement to significantly increase your potassium intake. You should speak with your physician first, especially if you have heart or kidney issues and if you are taking any medications. Extremely high potassium levels can in fact be deadly. Bear in mind that the participants in this study increased their potassium intake simply by replacing their more processed snacks with more fruits, vegetables, and nuts - something you can easily do yourself.

Potassium-Enriched Salt Reduces Risk of Death

If taking potassium can help reduce one's blood pressure, what about using salt substitutes? Many are made with potassium chloride and other potassium salts, so might using them help?

In a study looking at potassium and blood pressure, researchers in Taiwan, where the average daily intake of sodium in elderly men is about 5 grams (5,000 mg) per day, sought to find out if using a salt substitute high in potassium would measurably affect the risk of death from heart disease.[9]

They performed the research at a nearby veteran's retirement home where each resident is assigned to receive his meals from one of five kitchens, all serving the same menu each day. Each kitchen serves two "squads" of veterans and each squad includes about 200 men. Two of the kitchens were chosen randomly to switch to a salt substitute which was half sodium chloride and half potassium chloride, while the other three kitchens continued using plain salt (all sodium chloride). Over the course of about 2 1/2 years (on average), the researchers noted the cause of death for all veterans who passed away during that period and were also able to note the cost of health care administered to the veterans.

Those men who were assigned to the salt substitute were less likely to die of heart-disease-related illnesses than those in the regular salt groups. Interestingly, this effect was most strongly seen after the veterans had been on the low-salt, high-potassium diet for 3 months. That reduced-sodium diet also resulted in lower expenditures for heart-disease-related health care: inpatient (hospital) treatment for those on the low sodium diet cost about 40% less than it did for those on the regular salt diet.

It's important to note that those veterans who participated in the study were not getting enough potassium in their diets before the study began, and the researchers were unable to determine with certainty whether their lower risk of death from heart disease was due to the potassium supplementation or the decrease in sodium. The veterans' diets were still high in sodium even when they were in the low-sodium group: their average daily intake was about 3.8 grams (3,800 milligrams), which is still high even if lower than their typical 5.2 grams.

It may be that switching to a salt substitute, even if that does not reduce your actual sodium intake under the recommended 2,000 milligrams per day, may still help you reduce your risk of death from heart disease. Given the increase in potassium this sort of change is something that you should speak with your doctor about, especially if you are on blood pressure or other prescription medications.

What is the DASH (Dietary Approaches to Stop Hypertension) Diet?

The recipes in this book and the Dr. Gourmet Web site grow out of Mediterranean diet research. There has been a great deal of information that has grown out of thousands of studies and, for the most part, the DASH Diet is the practical application of Mediterranean diet research. The studies in the 1970s and 1980s about Mediterranean diet laid the foundation for great quality nutrition research in the 1990s.

The result was a groundbreaking study of 459 adults age 22 years or older.[10] The primary goal was to look at how diet might influence blood pressure. Participants had systolic blood pressures (the top number) less than 160 and diastolic pressure (the bottom number) between 80 and 95. A total of 29% carried a diagnosis of hypertension, but none of those in the study was taking high blood pressure medications. Other characteristics of participants included:

- 50% female
- 60% African Americans (who have much higher rates of high blood pressure than other ethnicities)
- 27% were smokers.

Participants were divided into three groups:
- The control group was given a diet similar to what many Americans consumed

at the time, although it was lower in potassium, magnesium, and calcium.

- The second group was similar to the control but were given more fruits and vegetables
- The third group was the DASH diet.

This table outlines the DASH diet:

Food Group	Daily Servings	Serving Size	Choices	Notes
Grains, grain products	7–8	1 slice bread, 1 oz. dry cereal,† 1/2 cup cooked rice, pasta, or cereal	Whole wheat bread, English muffin, pita bread, bagel, cereals, grits, oatmeal, crackers, unsalted pretzels, popcorn	Major sources of energy and fiber
Vegetables	4–5	Serving sizes: 1 cup raw leafy vegetable, 1/2 cup cooked vegetable, 6 oz. vegetable juice	Tomatoes, potatoes, carrots, green peas, squash, broccoli, turnip greens, collards, kale, spinach, artichokes, green beans, lima beans, sweet potatoes	Rich sources of potassium, magnesium, and fiber
Fruits	4-5	Serving sizes: 6 oz. fruit juice, 1 medium fruit, 1/4 cup dried fruit, 1/2 cup fresh, frozen, or canned fruit	Apricots, bananas, dates, grapes, oranges, orange juice, grapefruit, grapefruit juice, mangoes, melons, peaches, pineapples, prunes, raisins, strawberries,	Important sources of potassium, magnesium, and fiber
Low-fat or fat-free dairy	2–3	Serving sizes: 8 oz. milk, 1 cup yogurt, 1 1/2 oz. cheese	Fat-free (skim) or low-fat (1%) milk, fat-free or low-fat buttermilk, fat-free or low-fat regular or frozen yogurt, low-fat and fat-free cheese	Major sources of calcium and protein
Meats, poultry, and fish	2 or less	Serving sizes: 3 oz. cooked meats, poultry, or fish	Select only lean meats; trim away visible fat; broil, roast, or boil, instead of frying; remove skin from poultry	Rich sources of protein and magnesium
Nuts, seeds, and dry beans	4–5 per week	Serving sizes: 1/3 cup or 1 1/2 oz. nuts, 2 Tbsp. or 1/2 oz. seeds, 1/2 cup cooked dry beans	Almonds, filberts, mixed nuts, peanuts, walnuts, sunflower seeds, kidney beans, lentils, peas	Rich sources of energy, magnesium, potassium, protein, and fiber

Food Group	Daily Servings	Serving Size	Choices	Notes
Fats and oils	2–3	Serving sizes: 1 tsp. soft margarine, 1 Tbsp. low-fat mayonnaise, 2 Tbsp. light salad dressing, 1 tsp. vegetable oil	Soft margarine, low-fat mayonnaise, light salad dressing, vegetable oil (eg, olive, corn, canola, safflower)	DASH has 27% of calories as fat, including that in or added to foods
Sweets	5 per week	Serving sizes: 1 Tbsp. sugar, 1 Tbsp. jelly or jam, 1/2 oz. jelly beans, 8 oz. lemonade	Maple syrup, sugar, jelly, jam, fruit-flavored gelatin, jelly beans, hard candy, fruit punch, sorbet, ices	Sweets should be low in fat

The results were pretty fantastic:

> DASH diet lowered systolic blood pressure by an average of 6 mm Hg
>
> DASH diet lowered diastolic pressure by about 3 mm Hg.
>
> The Fruit and vegetable diet also lowered blood pressure about 3 mm Hg systolic and 2 mm Hg diastolic.

For those with stage 1 hypertension (blood pressure 140/90–159/99 mm Hg):

> DASH diet reduced systolic blood pressure by an average of 11 mm Hg
>
> DASH diet reduced diastolic blood pressure by 6 mm Hg
>
> The lower blood pressures were seen within 2 weeks of starting the diets.

I lecture all the time about diet and often speak about how I believe that we have two considerations when talking about diet and nutrition. One is weight loss and that is, for the most part, about the number of calories consumed vs. those burned (calories in < calories out = weight loss).

The other part of the dialogue is about the quality of those calories. In this case, that means more whole grains, vegetables, fruits, nuts, seeds, dried beans, low-fat dairy, lean meats (and less meat) and quality fats.

The interesting thing about this study was that people didn't lose much weight (that wasn't the goal of the study), but as you can see they had a dramatic improvement in their blood pressures. We see these same sorts of results when looking at Mediterranean style diet.

The DASH Diet and the Mediterranean Diet

The DASH Diet is so successful because its foundations are drawn from research on the Mediterranean diet. Many of the researchers who took part in the initial DASH study were the same who detailed the benefits of the Mediterranean diet. If you look at them side by side it's easy to see how similar they are:

DASH Diet	Mediterranean Diet
Grains: whole grain products	Grains: whole grain products
Fruit	Fruit and Nuts
Vegetables	Vegetables
Low-fat or fat-free dairy	Low-fat or fat-free dairy
Meats, poultry and fish	Less meat and lean meat
	More fish
Nuts, seeds and dry beans	Legumes (note nuts above with fruit)
Fats and oils outlined	More unsaturated and less saturated fat
Sweets	
	Alcohol in moderation

Lower Sodium Equals Lower Blood Pressure

The results of the initial DASH study found that those following the diet had both lower systolic and diastolic blood pressures for those without high blood pressure. The effect in those with hypertension was even greater, with blood pressure reductions of around 11 points.[11] This was profound information at the time, but as researchers are prone to do, they thought that they might be able to do better.

At the time there were questions about whether lowering the sodium content in the DASH diet might be even more effective. The three diets in the DASH diet study contained approximately 3,000 mg sodium per day. A follow up trial, the DASH – Sodium study, was devised with diets similar to the control diet and the DASH diet in the previous study.

Each diet plan was, however, designed with three levels of sodium – the original 3,000 mg per day as well as 2,400 mg and 1,500 mg levels. The study was designed as a crossover trial where each of the 6 groups followed the diet for a month and changed diets at the beginning of the following month. This intervention strategy insures that the results of each plan are valid in all the participants.

Control Diet	DASH – Sodium Diet
3,000 mg	3,000 mg
2,400 mg	2,400 mg
1,500 mg	1,500 mg

The original DASH diet, with 3,000 mg sodium, lowered blood pressure in all of the participants to the levels seen in previous studies. Lowering sodium intake to 2,400 mg/day effectively reduced blood pressure for all participants.

Sodium intakes at 1,500 mg per day, however, lowered blood pressure by twice as much with a reduction of 8.9 points (systolic) and 4.5 points (diastolic). Once again, the effect was greater in those who were already hypertensive with a drop in blood pressure of 11.5 points (systolic) and 5.7 points (diastolic).

The challenge for the DASH diets was that both of the studies were designed by giving the participants pre-prepared food. That level of control makes it easier for researchers to prove that a diet works, but the real test would be to find out whether simply teaching people how to eat would offer the same benefit. In a third trial researchers divided study participants into three groups:

Advice-only (control): Participants received a single education session with printed handouts.

Established recommendations: This group received behavioral counseling of 18 sessions with trained interventionists (typically registered dietitians) over 6 months using recommendations for non-pharmacologic management of hypertension including:

      reduced sodium intake

      increased physical activity

      limited alcohol intake,

      weight loss

Established-plus-DASH: The final group also had 18 counseling sessions based on the established recommendations plus the DASH diet.

The results were similar to the controlled studies with those following the DASH diet showing a 25% reduction in the number having high blood pressure. Even better, 35% of those who with hypertension at the beginning of the study were more likely to have optimal control of their pressures.

Outcome	Baseline	Advice Only	Established Recommendations	Established + DASH Diet
% with Hypertension	37	26	17	12
% with Optimal control	0	19	30	35

These studies were amongst the first large scale controlled trials to prove the impact of diet on high blood pressure. The best part is that the research has been repeated with both DASH and Mediterranean diet plans giving you great options in getting healthier and staying healthy.

How to Read Nutrition Labels

Nutrition Facts	
Serving size	1 cup (228g)
Servings Per Container	2
Calories 120	Calories from Fat 110
	% Daily Value*
Total Fat 12 g	18 %
Saturated Fat 0 g	15 %
Trans Fat 0 g	
Monounsaturated Fat 0 g	
Cholesterol 30 mg	10 %
Sodium 470 mg	20 %
Total Carbohydrate 31 g	10 %
Dietary Fiber 0 g	0 %
Sugars 5 g	
Protein 5 g	
Vitamin A 4 %	Vitamin C 2 %
Calcium 20 %	Iron 4 %

*Percent Daily Values are based on a 2,000 calorie diet. Your Daily Values may be higher or lower depending on your calorie needs.

	Calories:	2,000	2,500
Total Fat	Less than	65g	80g
Sat Fat	Less than	20g	25g
Cholesterol	Less than	300mg	300mg
Sodium	Less than	2,400mg	2,400mg
Total Carbohydrate		375g	375g
Dietary Fiber		30g	30g

There was a time when the Nutrition Facts box on food labels didn't exist. The first book I wrote was mostly about how to read a food label, because before 1990 all that was required from food manufacturers was simply a listing of ingredients. The only way to know if what you were buying might be healthy or not was that the ingredients were listed in order of amount by weight.

This is still the case and when you see that sugar is the first ingredient listed you know that there's more sugar by weight than any of the other ingredients. But we now, of course, have a lot more information. It can still be a bit of a challenge, however, if you don't know a lot about nutrition. Here's a guide on how to read the Nutrition Facts box.

The first step is to break the Nutrition Facts box down into sections.

The first section contains the serving size and the number of servings in the package. This is the place where food manufacturers try to trick you because a lot of smaller packages are realistically only a single serving, but they will list it as 2 or 3 servings. (The cynic in me believes that this is done to make you believe that the food is healthier than you might other- wise believe.)

A good example of this is a 16 ounce bottle of juice. Juice can be a healthy choice, but most folks will drink the whole bottle. It seems reasonable but it's actually a lot of calories. A quick glance at the Nutrition Facts shows that there are only 120 calories in a serving, but if you don't look closely you might not notice that there are two servings in the bottle, adding up to 240 calories in the whole bottle.

The next step is to look at the serving size and how many servings are in that package.

Below that is the number of calories per serving. Simple enough, but always be suspect and look back at the number of servings per container. This section also tells you how many of those calories are from fat. In this case it's pretty high. This works as a good guide about whether what you are getting ready to eat contains too much fat.

The third section is the one that shows you how much fat, cholesterol and sodium are in the package. There is also a breakdown of the fats by type - Saturated and Trans Fats. Note that this food contains Trans Fat. Put those back on the shelf. You want a food or ingredient with zero (0) Trans Fats.

For sodium the percentages listed on packages are based on a total daily intake of 2,400 milligrams (mg). This is a much lower sodium intake than most of us are eating today, with the average American consuming up to 6,000 mg per day. There are estimates that place intake much higher -- in the 10,000 mg per day range for western diets (that's ten GRAMS of sodium).

Even though we have much better research on this now, it turns out that the guideline of 2,400 mg was a pretty good target. For those simply trying to eat healthier, the American Heart Association recommends 2,300 mg per day (this is about the amount in a teaspoon of salt). Most physicians have their patients with conditions such as congestive heart failure (CHF) and hypertension eat less, however, with a target of less than 2,000 mg and often 1,500 mg per day.

The easiest way to approach this is to divide your day into meals with targets at breakfast and lunch under 500 mg sodium and dinner under 1,000 mg for those who are aiming for about 2,000 mg per day. For those on a 1,500 mg per day plan, a good breakdown might be 400 mg for breakfast, the same for lunch, and 500 to 600 mg at dinner. Look at the Nutrition Facts on any package of food and add the total milligrams of sodium for the foods that you are eating at a meal.

This section has similar information on carbohydrates and protein. One key in this section is to focus on the amount of sugars. While a lot of foods are high in natural sugars - fruit, juices and the like - it's a good idea to limit the amount of sugar in most cases - but especially in any processed foods.

The bottom is best for you to use as a guide. It's where you can find the quick and easy information. This section is the "Percent Daily Value" - the percentage of fat, cholesterol, sodium, etc. that you should have in a day. In this example the food has 18% of the total fat you should have for the day (these percentages are based on a 2,000 calorie diet).

As previously mentioned, the % Daily Value of sodium is based on 2,400 mg of sodium per day. Your target may be lower, so the percentage may fool you and be lower than you think. To get your % daily value, divide by the amount of sodium per day recommended by your doctor.

The bottom section gives you a guide as to those recommended amounts. Unfortunately, not a lot of folks should be eating 2,000 or more calories per day, so you have to make adjustments based on your needs.

Sodium in Processed Foods

Most of the salt in our diets comes from the processed food we eat. Several countries, including Finland, the United Kingdom and Australia, have instituted government and food-industry-led strategies to reduce the amount of sodium in processed foods, with some success: the UK has managed to reduce their overall average salt intake by about 10% (from 9.5 to 8.6 grams per day). The question is, how consistent is the nutrition information found across various processed foods?

Recently a team in Australia assessed the amount of salt in over 7,000 processed foods sold in Australia as part of their effort to gather information on the current status of their food industry.[12]

The foods that were evaluated came from 10 food groups, 33 food categories and 90 food subcategories, ranging from canned fruits to processed meats to sauces and spreads. A specific food was included in their list only one time: multiple instances of the same food, because of different packaging or serving sizes, were excluded. The researchers then recorded the brand and product name, the serving size, the amount of sodium per serving and the amount of sodium per 100 grams (or 100 milliliters, when the food was a liquid).

The outcome of their research shows not only the average amount of sodium in different foods across the various brands, but also shows the range of sodium amounts within each food. Take bacon as an example. There are 47 different products within the "Bacon" category, representing 92% of the market share for that product. While the average amount of sodium in 100 grams of bacon (about 3.5 ounces) is about 1,243 milligrams, the variation in the amount of sodium across bacon brands is enormous, ranging from 920 milligrams to 1,950 milligrams.

For most categories, the researchers discovered that the sodium level for those products with the highest amounts of sodium were at least 50% higher than the sodium levels for the comparable products with the least amount of sodium. The foods with the highest average salt content were sauces and spreads, while the foods with the lowest average salt content were canned fruits. The food with the highest average salt content (6,100 milligrams per 100 milliliter) was stocks or broths (which should explain why so many of Dr. Gourmet recipes specify low sodium or no salt added chicken, beef or vegetable broths).

The researchers' intentions in collecting this data is to help guide a national salt-reduction program. Such over-arching initiatives haven't taken root here in the United States as of yet. Your take-home message here should be that there can be wide variations in salt content in many of the foods you purchase, so you should compare packages and choose the brand with the lowest amount of sodium.

Sodium and Mood

There is research to show that low levels of dehydration can affect people's mood - causing higher levels of anger or hostility, fatigue, and feeling that a given task is more difficult to perform. At the same time following a Mediterranean-style diet also appears to be good for your mood, improving feelings of contentedness, vigor and alertness. A recent study published in the journal *Nutrition* suggests that a diet with lower levels of sodium may also have a positive effect on your mood.[13]

Australian researchers recruited 95 postmenopausal women to participate in a 14-week diet study. The participants were randomly assigned to one of two diets: a "Vitality Diet" which was a standard DASH diet enriched with a daily serving of lean red meat, or a "Healthy Diet," which focused on lower fat, higher complex carbohydrates, and limiting red meat intake. The Vitality Diet had higher targets for fruit and vegetable intake than the Healthy Diet: four servings of each were the recommendation versus only 2 each for the Healthy Diet.

The women kept a food diary throughout the study and responded to weekly standardized questionnaires designed to assess their mood. Urine tests measured the women's sodium and potassium intake, so that the researchers knew that the Vitality Diet group was meeting their lower sodium targets while the Healthy Diet group's sodium levels remained the same as at the start of the study.

The researchers found that all of the participants' overall mood scores improved over the course of the 14 weeks of the study. But there were two very interesting differences between the two groups: first, the measured levels of anger in the Vitality Diet group decreased more than in the Healthy Diet group, and the higher levels of meat intake in the Vitality Diet group seemed to lead to lower levels of confusion and depression.

The researchers note that it is difficult to show causality between diet and mood, but this is by no means the only study finding a link between mood and diet. What's clear is that a diet that includes more vegetables and fruit and a lower level of sodium can help keep you happier as well as healthier.

About MSG (Monosodium Glutamate)

Beyond the amount of sodium that is in foods containing MSG there are other reasons to make sure you are avoiding foods containing this additive.

A couple of years ago researchers in North Carolina looked at 752 middle-aged Chinese persons, of whom 82% used MSG regularly. They saw a clear relationship between using MSG and being overweight. The drawback of that study is that it included a relatively small population, all from rural villages. The good news is that a much stronger study supports the initial findings.[14]

This study made use of data gathered through the China Health and Nutrition Survey, which includes people from across China, from high-income and low-income cities as well as suburban and rural areas. The study began collecting data in 1991 and included over 7100 healthy men and women who were between the ages of 18 and 65. In addition to demographic data such as height, weight, education and activity level, the study included detailed information collected about both household and individual food consumption. That consumption was assessed not only by participants recalling what they ate (which is prone to error), but also by actually visiting the participants' homes and performing an inventory of all the food and ingredients there and comparing the changes in that inventory at the beginning and end of the day for three consecutive days.

Further, MSG intake could be directly measured because it is added as an ingredient, just as you might add pepper or another spice. Soy sauce, another common ingredient, contains a known amount of MSG and was also easily weighed.

The average level of daily MSG intake was calculated for each person and correlated with their Body Mass Index. After stratifying average daily MSG intake into five increasing levels, the researchers could see that even when taking into account each person's activity level, the amount of fat or carbohydrates in their diet, and the average total number of calories they consumed each day, those who ate the most MSG were 33% more likely to be overweight than those who ate the least.

We don't know exactly why this association exists, but the current theory is that MSG influences the body's ability to manage its energy balance through interfering with the activity of the hormone leptin in the body. As far as I'm concerned, like High Fructose Corn Syrup, the presence of Monosodium Glutamate in a food should signal to you that it's overly-processed and not something you want to be eating. Better to enhance the flavors of your food by using great quality ingredients - not by adding an artificial flavor enhancer.

What Not To Eat for Lunch

Baloney.

It's so easy to beat up on this seemingly innocent little cold cut but it just has to be done. This is the prototype of what you should not be eating at lunch. That is, you should avoid bologna and while you're at it pretty much all cold cuts. The highly processed luncheon meats that are sold today are for the most part poor choices.

"But Dr. Tim," you might say. "A slice of bologna has only 87 calories." That's true, but about 72 of those are from fat and about a third of that innocent little slice is saturated fat. Pair this with a slice of American cheese and a glob of mayonnaise on white bread and you have what is wrong with the Western diet today. That innocent little piece of America comes in at 369 calories, 330 mg sodium and 20 grams of fat. Add a second slice of bologna and you can easily top 450 calories and 1,000 mg of sodium. (By the way, there's only 1 gram of fiber in this sandwich.)

"That's OK," you say. "I don't eat bologna. I 'Eat Fresh' and go to Subway for my sandwiches." Well, that's OK but you do have to be careful there also. The simplest Subway sandwiches are fairly healthy, but that applies to the basic 6 inch without cheese (which they will happily throw in for free) on their 9-grain wheat bread with lettuce, tomatoes, onions, green peppers and cucumbers. A Turkey Breast sandwich (no cheese) is 280 calories, but it contains a whopping 920 mg of sodium. This is their most basic sandwich and things that you feel might be good choices aren't. The Subway signature 6" BMT sub comes in at 450 calories, 20 grams of fat and a whopping 1,730 mg of sodium.

In short, it's best to be really careful about your choice of cold cuts. That includes those made with turkey. It's fairly often that I have a patient come in and tell me that "It's OK, I'm having turkey bologna." That's better but not great. Cold cuts are the one package that you have to look at very closely. They will often be high in fat and almost always have way too much salt. But then there are also a lot of other ingredients you don't need. This is an ingredient list from a popular turkey bologna:

WHITE TURKEY, WATER, MODIFIED CORN STARCH, CONTAINS LESS THAN 2% OF POTASSIUM LACTATE, SALT, SUGAR, SODIUM PHOSPHATES, SODIUM DIACETATE, LEMON JUICE SOLIDS, SODIUM ASCORBATE, SODIUM NITRITE.

You just don't need all that stuff, and as they say, you don't want to know how sausage is made. That holds true for bologna and other cold cuts.

So what to do? I think that limiting your cold cuts to no more than once a week is a good start. Take leftovers from dinner instead if you can. You'll know that what you are having is better for you. If you do choose a deli sandwich or one from Subway, look carefully at the nutrition facts.

One great option is to make your lunch sandwich with leftovers. Make a great roast turkey breast on Sunday and use it for your sandwiches during the week. Pot Roast is another good option. Even if you don't have time to make your own, you'll be far better off picking up a rotisserie chicken and carving your own chicken for sandwiches.

What Not To Eat: Convenience Foods Edition

We review convenience meals on the Dr. Gourmet website. While I am not a fan of them, I do realize that folks are busy and challenged for time, so we try to look for the better choices to help you out. Most of the ones that we choose to put to the tasting panel come out of the freezer case, and there's a reason for that. When I look for foods on the aisles of the grocery store, what I find is so terrible that I can't even consider putting anyone through having to taste it. (Our motto is: "We eat it so you don't have to.")

I will use Hamburger Helper as the prototype (hey, there are others but it's such an easy target). While it's simple for people to focus on fast food as well as the super-sizing of meals at restaurants and soda as being the things that have caused the obesity epidemic, Hamburger Helper is equally to blame (OK, not all by itself but it is the model for bad food). There is nothing valuable about this product in any way. Let's look at the Nutrition Facts.

First, note that the serving size is one cup *as prepared*. Sadly, this is unlikely to be the serving that most people consume, but even if they did the quality of the calories is pretty darn poor.

There are 310 calories per "serving" and they are made up of mostly the white pasta. As such, there is less than 1 gram of fiber, even with 23 grams of total carbs. There's 810 mg of sodium in that cup serving, but very few other minerals, with essentially no iron and no calcium (even though it's supposed to contain cheese). In spite of the fact that this is labeled "cheeseburger" there's more sugar than cheese in the box.

This is like eating a cheeseburger with white bread, meat and cheese (kind of) but without anything that might be good like lettuce, tomatoes, onions or even pickles.

What you get instead are things you won't recognize:

Maltodextrin

Monosodium glutamate (yep, MSG)

Modified corn starch

Yellow Lakes 5 & 6 (artificial color)

Gum Arabic

Disodium gyanylate

Disodium Inosinate

(interestingly, no High Fructose Corn Syrup)

I realize that there are a lot of jokes about the food on grocery store shelves being "plastic." In some cases this isn't far from the truth. That's not to say that Hamburger Helper is made of plastic, but it has very little nutritional value – high calorie, high salt, low fiber and few valuable nutrients. It's not just Hamburger Helper, of course, and not foods that you haven't heard of. Dinty Moore products, Hormel Compleats meals, Campbell's soups, Swanson Chicken A La King.... There are just too many of them to list.

What not to eat? As a rule of thumb, don't select convenience meals that are not frozen and be cautious about those that are frozen, reading the labels very carefully.

Notes

1.   Cutler, J. A., Follmann, D. & Allender, P. S. Randomized trials of sodium reduction: an overview. *American Journal of Clinical Nutrition* 65, 643S–651S (1997).

2.   Gardener, H., Rundek, T., Wright, C. B., Elkind, M. S. V. & Sacco, R. L. Dietary Sodium and Risk of Stroke in the Northern Manhattan Study. *Stroke* 43, 1200–1205 (2012).

3.   Eufinger, S. C. et al. Habitual dietary sodium intake is inversely associated with coronary flow reserve in middle-aged male twins. *American Journal of Clinical Nutrition* 95, 572–579 (2012).

4.   AMA JOINT REPORT OF THE COUNCIL ON MEDICAL SERVICE AND THE COUNCIL ON SCIENCE AND PUBLIC HEALTH. 1–11 (2010).

5.   Bertino, M., Beauchamp, G. K. & Engelman, K. Long-term reduction in dietary sodium alters the taste of salt. *American Journal of Clinical Nutrition* 36, 1134–1144 (1982).

6.   Bolhuis, D. P. et al. A Salt Reduction of 50% in Bread Does Not Decrease Bread Consumption or Increase Sodium Intake by the Choice of Sandwich Fillings. *J Nutr* 141, 2249–2255 (2011).

7.   Batenburg, M. & van der Velden, R. Saltiness Enhancement by Savory Aroma Compounds. *Journal of Food Science* 76, S280–S288 (2011).

8.   Nowson, C. A., Morgan, T. O. & Gibbons, C. Decreasing dietary sodium while following a self-selected potassium-rich diet reduces blood pressure. *Journal of Nutrition* 133, 4118–4123 (2003).

9.   Chang, H.-Y. et al. Effect of potassium-enriched salt on cardiovascular mortality and medical expenses of elderly men. *American Journal of Clinical Nutrition* 83, 1289–1296 (2006).

10.   Appel, L. J. et al. A clinical trial of the effects of dietary patterns on blood pressure. DASH Collaborative Research Group. *New England Journal of Medicine* 336, 1117–1124 (1997).

11.   Sacks, F. M. et al. Effects on blood pressure of reduced dietary sodium and the Dietary Approaches to Stop Hypertension (DASH) diet. DASH-Sodium Collaborative Research Group. *New England Journal of Medicine* 344, 3–10 (2001).

12.   Webster, J. L., Dunford, E. K. & Neal, B. C. A systematic survey of the sodium contents of processed foods. *American Journal of Clinical Nutrition* 91, 413–420 (2010).

13.   D, S. J. T. P. & D, C. A. N. P. A moderate-sodium DASH-type diet improves mood in postmenopausal women. *Nutrition* 1–5 (2012).doi:10.1016/j.nut.2011.11.029

14.   He, K. et al. Association of monosodium glutamate intake with overweight in Chinese adults: the INTERMAP Study. *Obesity* (Silver Spring) 16, 1875–1880 (2008).

How to Use This Diet

The first step is to determine your target weight. Using the appropriate table (Men or Women) on the next page, find your height in the left column. Then read across the row for your Ideal Body Weight. This is an estimated target weight based on CDC and World Health Organization guidelines. There can be other factors in determining your goal weight, so it's important to check with your physician about what is a good target for you.

After you have identified an Ideal Body Weight, there is an estimate for the total caloric intake needed for weight loss (to get to that weight) as well as a maintenance diet (to maintain that weight once you've achieved your goal).

The table below translates your total daily caloric intake into the number of servings of each recipe you should be eating.

Calories	● Breakfast	▲ Lunch	◼ Dinner	Extras
1000	●	▲	◼	
1200	●	▲ ▲	◼	
1500	● ●	▲ ▲	◼	
1800	● ●	▲ ▲	◼ ◼	
2000	● ●	▲ ▲	◼ ◼	

Female

Height (in inches)	Ideal Body Weight	For weight Loss	Maintenance
60	105	1000	1200
61	110	1000	1200
62	115	1000	1200
63	120	1000	1200
64	125	1200	1500
65	130	1200	1500
66	135	1200	1500
67	140	1200	1500
68	145	1200	1500
69	150	1500	1800
70	155	1500	1800
71	160	1500	1800
72	165	1500	1800

Male

Height (in inches)	Ideal Body Weight	For weight Loss	Maintenance
60	106	1000	1200
61	112	1000	1200
62	118	1000	1200
63	124	1000	1200
64	130	1200	1500
65	136	1200	1500
66	142	1200	1500
67	148	1200	1500
68	154	1200	1800
69	160	1200	1800
70	166	1500	1800
71	172	1500	1800
72	178	1500	2000
73	184	1500	2000
74	190	1500	2000
75	196	1500	2000
76	202	1500	2000

More About the Recipes

Recipes and menus have been labeled with a circle, triangle or square so that you can swap them easily in case you're allergic to a particular food.

 The Circle recipes are for breakfast.

 Triangle recipes are for lunch.

 Squares are for dinner recipes or menus. Often a side dish is recommended with the main course for dinner, and that is included in the square (your serving). Side dishes, or Extras, have no shapes assigned for this reason.

One square is equivalent to two triangles. (That is, one serving of a dinner menu or meal is equivalent to two lunch servings.)

Each individual recipe is labeled with the number of servings it makes inside each shape. For instance, this square shows you that the recipe will serve 2:

Each recipe has the approximate time next to it. Here is a dinner recipe that will take about 45 minutes to prepare and will serve two:

Menus that take more than 30 minutes will usually have leftovers or are for special occasion meals.

The Rules

1. If you don't like a particular food and want to substitute one recipe for another, be sure to choose a recipe with the same number of servings (and time value). For instance, you could have Candied Carrots with your Creamy Mac and Cheese instead of the Herbed Zucchini. Or you could trade Oven Fried Chicken for the Thai Coconut Shrimp.

2. Shopping lists are provided for you, with all the ingredients needed for each week's menus. The plan is designed to run Sunday through Saturday so that you can shop on Saturday, although you can start any day you wish and adjust the menu days accordingly.

3. Take some time to read through the recipes and the plan on Saturday before going to the store. There may be ingredients or techniques that you are not familiar with, or you may need to marinate a recipe the night before it is to be served. Likewise, there are equipment lists for each week that can help you to make sure that you have all the gear needed.

4. The plan does call for making some food on Sunday afternoon or evening to eat during the week (those are usually recipes that take more than 30 minutes).

Breakfast and lunch, when not specified in the weekly menu, are outlined in the Breakfast and Lunch Guidelines with options for menus for both meals.

6. There are meals scheduled for eating out. The rule is that you can order **any entree and eat half of it.** The other half is eaten the following day for lunch.

7. Lastly, there is **no between meal snacking.** Patients have told me that the first week or two can be a little more difficult, so you can have a piece of fruit for a snack if you really need one.

A word or two about what to drink

For the first six weeks I recommend that you don't drink any alcohol that is not on the diet. Depending on your health condition your doctor may not want you to drink alcohol at all and you should check with him or her about this before having any alcoholic beverages. You will find that I feel alcohol can be good for you, but at first you should avoid it primarily due to the calories in wine, beer or mixed drinks. After you have reached your maintenance weight, drink in moderation, remembering that all alcohol has calories.

Coffee and tea are not bad for you, in my opinion, but many of us do drink too much and cutting back may be something you want to think about. If you use sugar, consider changing to Splenda® or another non-calorie product like stevia. If you use cream or half and half, switch to 2% milk. As far as other liquids go, you may drink pretty much anything that doesn't have calories. I am not much of a fan of sodas (diet or regular) but if you are going to have them, drink only calorie-free products. I do feel that you would be better off to eliminate them from your life and drink water.

Water is great for you and you almost can't drink too much. The idea that it can fill you up and help you eat less may actually be true. Either way, this is good stuff. For many of us it is an acquired taste after having been saturated with so many sodas and sugary drinks. Work on drinking less soda and more water.

Breakfast Guidelines

Option No. 1

Cereal with Milk (or Yogurt) and a piece of Fruit

Cereals should have about 100 - 150 calories in a serving. 1/2 cup of skim or 1% milk is ideal. Using a half cup of non-fat yogurt is even better.

Cereal	Amount per serving	Comment
Cheerios	1 cup (30 grams)	Multi-grain are best!
Kellogg's All-Bran Bran Buds	1/2 cup (45 grams)	
Kellogg's All-Bran Extra Fiber	1 cup	
Kellogg's All-Bran Original	1 cup	
Kellogg's Special K	1 cup (30 grams)	
Kellogg's Special K with Red Berries	1 cup (31 grams)	
Bite Size Shredded Wheat	1 cup (52 grams)	Not frosted
Raisin Bran	1 cup	
Total Whole Grain	1 cup	
Total Raisin Bran	1 cup	
Kashi Cinnamon Harvest	1 cup	
Kashi GoLEAN	1 cup (53 grams)	
Oatmeal	1/4 cup	(before cooking)
Cream of Wheat	1/4 cup	(before cooking)

A word about Cereal Bars:

Cereal bars are for emergencies only. Eating a granola bar for breakfast is not a good substitute. Many of them have a lot of added calories (usually as sugar).

Option No. 2

Breads and Protein and a piece of Fruit

Breads should be served with a protein. Select one from the bread choices, a topping for your bread and one choice from the protein list.

Breads	Amount	Comment
Slice of Whole Wheat Toast	One	Choose whole grain breads
Bagel	1/2 large bagel	
Whole wheat English Muffin	1 whole muffin	
Muffin from recipe @ drgourmet.com	One	
Toppings & Spreads for Breads	**Amount**	**Comment**
Choose one only		
Take Control Light Spread	2 tsp.	
Promise Buttery Spread Light	2 tsp.	
Smart Balance Light Buttery Spread	2 tsp.	(Omega Plus is better)
Preserves or Jam	2 tsp.	Look for "low sugar"
Reduced-fat Cream Cheese	2 tsp.	The "light" cream cheese is best for spreading. I don't much like the "fat free" version and use it mostly in baking
Take Control Light Spread and Syrup or honey	2 tsp. and 1 Tbsp.	Topping for pancakes or French Toast
Protein	**Amount**	**Comment**
1 Large Egg	One	Cook in as little fat as possible
Peanut Butter	2 Tbsp.	Use instead of other spreads
Low-fat cheese	1/2 ounce	
2%, 1% or Skim Milk	1/2 cup	
Non-fat Yogurt	1 cup	Choose yogurt with no added sugar

Lunch Guidelines

Sandwiches, defined:

- **Whole Sandwich** = 2 lunch servings (two triangles)

   2 slices whole wheat bread with 2 ounces lean meat OR 2 ounces reduced-fat cheese

- **Half Sandwich** = 1 lunch serving (one triangle)

   1 slice whole wheat bread with 1 ounce lean meat OR 1 ounce reduced-fat cheese

Meat & Cheese Choices (choose the lowest sodium products)

Reduced-fat Swiss

Reduced-fat Cheddar

Reduced-fat Monterey Jack

Goat Cheese

Lean Ham slices

Lean Turkey slices

2 Tbsp. Peanut Butter

Sandwich extras (put on as much as you like)

Sliced tomato

Sliced peppers

Onions

Lettuce

Spreads

Hellman's Extra Light Mayonnaise: 1 Tbsp.

Any Coarse Ground Mustard: 1 Tbsp.

Dijon Style Mustard: 1 Tbsp.

Your Favorite Chutney: 1 Tbsp.

Roasted Garlic: 2 cloves

Tapenade: 1 Tbsp.

Leftovers

Remember, a lunch serving is one-half of a leftover dinner serving.

Weekly Meal Plans

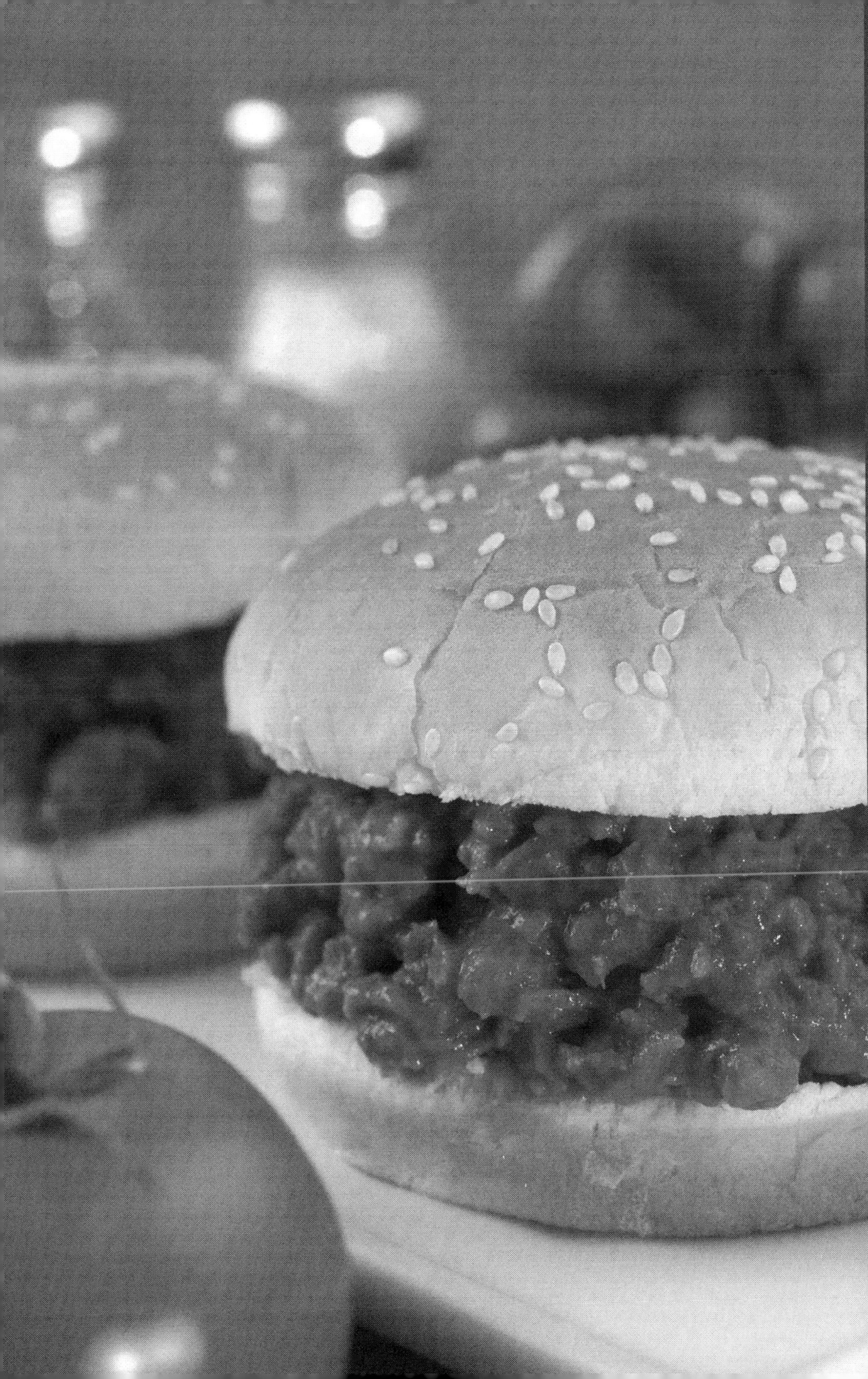

Week 1

	● Breakfast	▲ Lunch	■ Dinner	To Do
Week 1 Meal Plan				
Sunday	4 Servings Pecan Peach Muffins	4 Lunch Servings	2 Servings Ginger Chicken Satay with Peanut Sauce with Coconut Rice	Make Pecan Peach Muffins
Monday	2 Breakfast Servings, 2 Servings Pecan Peach Muffins	4 Lunch Servings	2 Servings Ginger Chicken Satay with Peanut Sauce with Coconut Rice	
Tuesday	4 Servings Healthy Strawberry Banana Smoothie	4 Lunch Servings Ginger Chicken Satay with Peanut Sauce	2 Servings Eggplant Risotto (double the recipe)	
Wednesday	4 Servings Cereal for Breakfast	4 Lunch Servings Eggplant Risotto	2 Servings Whitefish in Foil with Vegetables and Tomato Sauce	
Thursday	4 Servings Healthy Tropical Melon Smoothie	4 Lunch Servings Eggplant Risotto	2 Servings Mustard Cornmeal Crusted Fish with Plain Mashed Potatoes and Maple Sage Carrots	
Friday	4 Servings Healthy Toasted Oatmeal	4 Lunch Servings	2 Servings Mustard Cornmeal Crusted Fish with Plain Mashed Potatoes and Maple Sage Carrots	Make Blueberry Muffins
Saturday	4 Servings Blueberry Muffins	4 Lunch Servings	2 Servings Pasta Fagioli with Chicken	

Week 1 Grocery List

Produce

1 knob fresh ginger
1 bunch cilantro
1 bunch fresh basil
4 Cups fresh strawberries
1 1/2 lbs. cantaloupe
2 servings choice of fruit
4 bananas
1 pint blueberries
1 head garlic
3 onions
2 large eggplants
8 ounces cherry or grape tomatoes
4 spears asparagus
1 carrot
4 lbs. baby carrots
1 small green bell pepper
1 small red bell pepper
4 medium crimini mushrooms
1 lb. Yukon gold potatoes
1 bunch celery

Dairy

2 large eggs
1 qt. non-fat buttermilk
2 16-ounce tubs non-fat yogurt
5 ounces Parmigiano-Reggiano
4 ounces fresh mozzarella
1 qt. 2% milk
1 stick unsalted butter
1 tub Promise Buttery Spread Light or Smart Balance Light Spread

Meat/Fish

1 1/2 lbs. boneless skinless chicken breast
8 ounces boneless skinless chicken thighs
2 4-ounce halibut filets
4 4-ounce red snapper filets (or other whitefish)

Pantry Items

olive oil
extra virgin olive oil
pure vanilla extract
granular Splenda or stevia
light brown sugar
pure maple syrup
honey
all purpose flour
whole wheat flour
wheat germ
quick oats
coarse ground yellow cornmeal
1/4 Cup chopped pecans
sesame oil
2 15-ounce cans reduced-fat (lite) unsweetened coconut milk
jasmine rice
arborio rice
cereal of your choice (see list)
tomato paste
coarse ground mustard
low sodium chicken broth
low sodium soy sauce
smooth peanut butter
1 15-ounce can no salt added white beans
2 15-ounce cans no salt added navy beans
2 15-ounce cans no salt added diced tomatoes
8 ounces whole wheat pasta
salt
ground black pepper
baking powder
baking soda
ground nutmeg
dried tarragon
dried oregano
dried basil
dried rosemary
dried sage
dried red pepper flakes

Miscellaneous

8 ounces frozen peaches
12 wooden skewers
aluminum foil
mango juice
papaya juice (may substitute mango juice)
2 servings choice of fruit
white wine
2 Breakfast Servings
24 Lunch Servings

Week 2

Week 2 Meal Plan

	● Breakfast	▲ Lunch	■ Dinner	To Do
Sunday	4 Servings Omelet	4 Lunch Servings	2 Servings Pasta Fagioli with Chicken	
Monday	2 Breakfast Servings 2 Servings Blueberry Muffins	4 Lunch Servings Pasta Fagioli with Chicken	2 Servings Mussels with Saffron Broth	
Tuesday	4 Servings Cereal for Breakfast	4 Lunch Servings	2 Servings Vegetarian Corn and Black Bean Taco Salad	Make Banana Nut Muffins
Wednesday	4 Servings Banana Nut Muffins	4 Lunch Servings	2 Servings Fish Sandwiches with Sun Dried Tomato Tartar Sauce	
Thursday	2 Breakfast Servings 2 Servings Banana Nut Muffins	4 Lunch Servings	Eat Out - Fish	Make Banana Nut Bread
Friday	4 Servings Banana Nut Bread	4 Lunch Servings	2 Servings Roasted Southwestern Acorn Squash	
Saturday	4 Servings Yam and Leek Tortilla	4 Lunch Servings	2 Servings Beef Tips in Brown Gravy	

Week 2 Grocery List

Produce
- ◆ 3 large bananas
- ◆ 4 servings choice of fruit
- ◆ 3 green bell peppers
- ◆ 6 fresh basil leaves
- 2 lbs yams
- 1 large shallot
- ◆ 2 carrots
- ◆ 1 rib celery
- ◆ 3 lb. onions
- 2 ears corn
- 2 heads iceberg lettuce
- 3 large tomatoes
- ◆ 2 red bell peppers
- 2 Tbsp fresh chives
- 2 large leeks
- 1 large acorn squash
- ◆ 1 clove garlic
- ◆ 1 bunch cilantro leaves
- 1 lb button mushrooms

Dairy
- ◆ unsalted butter
- ◆ 19 large eggs
- ◆ 1/2 ounce Parmigiano-Reggiano
- 1 ounce goat cheese
- ◆ 2 Cups 2% milk
- 4 ounces reduced fat Monterey Jack cheese
- 3 ounces regular Monterey Jack cheese
- 6 Tbsp. reduced fat sour cream
- ◆ 3 Tbsp. Promise Buttery Spread Light or Take Control Light
- ◆ 1/2 Cup non-fat buttermilk

Meat/Fish
- 1 lb. top round or other lean beef
- 2 lbs. mussels
- 4 4-ounce white fish filets (grouper, cod, or halibut)

Bakery
- 4 whole wheat hamburger buns

Pantry Items
- 4 Cups cereal of your choice (see list)
- 3 15-ounce cans no salt added black beans
- ◆ 1/2 Cup olive oil
- ◆ 1 tsp. pure vanilla extract
- ◆ 1 1/2 Cups Splenda or stevia
- ◆ 3/4 Cup chopped pecans
- ◆ 2 1/4 Cups all purpose white flour
- ◆ 1 1/4 Cups whole wheat flour
- ◆ 1/2 Cup wheat germ
- reduced-fat mayonnaise
- Worcestershire sauce
- cornstarch
- unsalted corn tortilla chips
- ◆ 4 tsp. light brown sugar
- pickle relish
- sun dried tomato paste
- ◆ 8 ounces whole wheat spaghetti
- 20 threads saffron
- chili powder
- cumin
- ◆ 2 tsp. salt
- ◆ 3 tsp. baking powder
- ◆ 3/4 tsp. baking soda
- ground cinnamon
- ◆ 1/2 tsp. ground nutmeg
- dried thyme leaves
- ◆ 1/2 tsp. dried oregano

Misc.
- ◆ 1/2 Cup white wine
- 2/3 Cup frozen peas
- 4 breakfast servings
- 24 lunch servings

◆ indicates previously purchased - check pantry first

Week 3

Week 3 Meal Plan			
	● Breakfast	▲ Lunch	■ Dinner	To Do
Sunday	4 Servings Blueberry Pancakes	4 Lunch Servings	2 Servings Sweet Red Pepper Barbecue Tuna with Jasmine Rice	
Monday	4 Servings Healthy Tropical Melon Smoothie	4 Lunch Servings	2 Servings Sweet Red Pepper Barbecue Tuna with Jasmine Rice	Make Blueberry Muffins
Tuesday	4 Servings Blueberry Muffins	4 Lunch Servings Sweet Red Pepper Barbecue Tuna	2 Servings Seared Halibut with Basil Oil with Orzo with Tapenade and Pan Grilled Asparagus	
Wednesday	2 Breakfast Servings 2 Servings Blueberry Muffins	4 Lunch Servings	2 Servings Polynesian Chicken with Coconut Rice and Thai Cucumber Salad	Make Banana Nut Muffins
Thursday	4 Servings Banana Nut Muffins	4 Lunch Servings	2 Servings Polynesian Chicken with Coconut Rice and Thai Cucumber Salad	
Friday	2 Breakfast Servings 2 Servings Banana Nut Muffins	4 Lunch Servings	2 Servings Cumin Dusted Flank Steak with Black Beans	
Saturday	4 Servings Creole Frittata	4 Lunch Servings	2 Servings Seared Tuna with Asparagus Salsa with Baked Sweet Potato	

Week 3 Grocery List

Produce

- ◆ 1/2 Cup blueberries
- ◆ 1/2 Cup fresh blueberries (or strawberries or blackberries)
- ◆ 2 red bell peppers
- 24 ounces cantaloupe
- ◆ 3 large bananas
- ◆ 1/2 Cup fresh basil leaves
- ◆ 2 shallots
- ◆ 1 red bell pepper
- 2 yellow bell peppers
- 1 1/2 lbs. asparagus spears
- ◆ 1 clove garlic
- 1 Cup pineapple (diced)
- 3 limes
- 1 red onion
- 2 medium onions
- 1 bunch green onions
- 2 large cucumbers
- ◆ 1/4 Cup cilantro leaves
- ◆ 1 small tomato
- 1 bunch fresh oregano
- 4 6-ounce yams

Dairy

- ◆ 2 1/2 Cups non-fat buttermilk
- 1/2 Cup egg substitute
- ◆ 1/2 Cup Promise Buttery Spread Light or Take Control Light
- ◆ 2 1/4 Cups non-fat yogurt
- ◆ 10 large eggs
- 4 ounces reduced fat cheddar cheese
- ◆ 4 tsp. unsalted butter
- 2 ounces goat cheese

Meat/Fish

- 1 lb. boneless skinless chicken breast
- 2 4-ounce flank steak filets
- 10 4-ounce tuna steaks
- 2 4-ounce filets halibut

Pantry Items

- ◆ 4 Cups all purpose white flour
- ◆ 1 1/2 Cup Splenda or stevia
- ◆ 3 tsp. pure vanilla extract
- pure maple syrup
- ◆ 2 Tbsp. peach preserves
- light brown sugar
- 1/2 Cup cider vinegar
- ◆ 1 Tbsp. Worcestershire sauce
- ◆ 2 1/2 Cups jasmine rice
- ◆ 1 Cup whole wheat flour
- ◆ 1/2 Cup wheat germ
- ◆ 1/4 Cup extra virgin olive oil
- ◆ 3 Tbsp. olive oil
- capers
- ◆ 3 Tbsp. low-sodium soy sauce
- canola or grapeseed oil
- 1/2 Cup pineapple juice
- 1 Tbsp. honey
- ◆ 1 Cup reduced-fat (lite) un-sweetened coconut milk
- rice vinegar
- raw peanuts
- ◆ 1/4 Cup chopped pecans
- ◆ 1 15-ounce can no salt added black beans
- ◆ 4 tsp. baking powder
- 3 tsp. salt
- dry mustard
- ◆ 1 1/2 tsp. chili powder
- paprika
- ◆ 1/2 tsp. baking soda
- 1 tsp. ground ginger
- Tabasco or other hot sauce
- ◆ 1/2 tsp. ground cinnamon
- ◆ 1/4 tsp. ground nutmeg
- ◆ 2 tsp. ground cumin
- cayenne pepper
- 2 tsp. no salt added Creole or Cajun seasoning blend

Misc.

- ◆ 1 1/3 Cup mango or papaya juice
- 4 ounces orzo pasta
- tapenade
- 4 breakfast servings
- 24 lunch servings

◆ indicates previously purchased - check pantry first

Week 4 Meal Plan			
	● Breakfast	▲ Lunch	■ Dinner	To Do
Sunday	4 Servings Apple Cinnamon Bread	4 Lunch Servings	Eat Out - Fish	Make Roasted Garlic for Cream of Potato Soup on Tuesday
Monday	4 Servings Apple Cinnamon Bread	4 Lunch Servings	2 Servings Pork Chops with Garlic Sauce with Mashed Yams and Shredded Brussels Sprouts	Double the Pork Chops with Garlic Sauce recipe to use as sandwiches. Roast garlic.
Tuesday	4 Servings Healthy Toasted Oatmeal	4 Lunch Servings Sandwiches made with 2 ounces each leftover pork	2 Servings Cream of Potato Soup with Roasted Garlic and Zucchini Salad	
Wednesday	4 Servings Cereal for Breakfast	4 Lunch Servings Sandwiches made with 2 ounces each leftover pork	2 Servings Cream of Potato Soup with Roasted Garlic and Zucchini Salad	
Thursday	4 Servings Healthy Strawberry Banana Smoothie	4 Lunch Servings	2 Servings Basque Chicken Stew	
Friday	4 Servings Healthy Strawberry Banana Smoothie	4 Lunch Servings	2 Servings Basque Chicken Stew	Make Red Pepper Pesto
Saturday	4 Servings Pecan Sweet Potato Bread	4 Lunch Servings	2 Servings Gnocchi with Red Pepper Pesto and Caesar Salad	

Week 4 Grocery List

Produce

2 large apples
◆ 8 heads garlic
◆ 1 1/2 lb. yams
◆ 1 large shallot
1 lb. brussels sprouts
◆ 2 white onions
12 ounces Idaho potatoes
1 1/2 lbs. Yukon gold potatoes
4 pints fresh strawberries
◆ 4 bananas
◆ 1 green bell pepper
◆ 1 yellow bell pepper
◆ 2 red bell peppers
8 ounces grape or cherry tomatoes
1 bunch fresh basil
2 lemons
4 servings choice of fruit
2 heads romaine lettuce (1 per salad)
1 lb. zucchini

Dairy

◆ 9 large eggs
◆ 1/2 Cup Promise Buttery Spread Light or Take Control Light
◆ 1 Cup non-fat buttermilk
◆ 4 tsp. unsalted butter
1 qt. 2% milk
4 ounces smoked gouda cheese
◆ 3 8-ounce tubs non-fat yogurt
◆ 2 1/2 ounces Parmigiano-Reggiano cheese

Meat/Fish

4 4-ounce pork chops
1 lb. boneless skinless chicken thighs

Pantry Items

◆ 3/4 Cup pecans
◆ 3/4 Cup maple syrup
◆ 1 1/2 Cups Splenda or Stevia
1/2 Cup unsweetened applesauce
◆ 1 1/2 tsp. pure vanilla extract
◆ 3 1/4 Cups all purpose white flour
◆ 1 1/2 Cups whole wheat flour
◆ 1/2 Cup wheat germ
◆ 2 Cups quick oats
◆ 4 Cups cereal of your choice (see list)
◆ 3/4 Cup olive oil
◆ 1/2 Cup extra virgin olive oil
balsamic vinegar
white wine vinegar
1 tin anchovy filets
1 15-ounce can no salt added diced tomatoes
2 Tbsp. reduced-fat croutons
Dijon mustard
◆ 2 Tbsp. honey
◆ 1 1/2 Cups low sodium chicken broth
◆ 8 tsp. light brown sugar
◆ 3/4 Cup pine nuts
1 Cup lentils
◆ 1 1/2 tsp. ground cinnamon
◆ 3 tsp. salt
◆ 4 tsp. baking powder
◆ 1 tsp. baking soda
◆ 1/4 tsp. dried rosemary
◆ 1/4 tsp. saffron threads
paprika
◆ 1/8 tsp. ground nutmeg
◆ 1/2 tsp. ground black pepper
◆ 1 tsp. dried marjoram

Misc.

◆ 1/2 Cup white wine
◆ 4 Cups mango juice

◆ indicates previously purchased - check pantry first

Week 5 Meal Plan			
	● **Breakfast**	▲ **Lunch**	■ **Dinner**	**To Do**
Sunday	4 Servings Ginger-bread	4 Lunch Servings	2 Servings Broccoli Cheese Soup with Zucchini Salad	
Monday	4 Servings Ginger-bread	4 Lunch Servings	2 Servings Broccoli Cheese Soup with Zucchini Salad	
Tuesday	4 Servings Healthy Toasted Oatmeal	4 Lunch Servings Broccoli Cheese Soup	2 Servings Chicken with Creamy Red Pepper Flakes Sauce	
Wednesday	4 Servings Healthy Strawberry Banana Smoothie	4 Lunch Servings	2 Servings Quick Cheeseburger Mac with Caesar Salad	Make Banana Nut Muffins
Thursday	4 Servings Banana Nut Muffins	4 Lunch Servings	2 Servings Quick Cheeseburger Mac with Caesar Salad	Roast Garlic
Friday	2 Breakfast Servings 2 Banana Nut Muffins	4 Lunch Servings Quick Cheeseburger Mac	2 Servings Poached Salmon with Roasted Garlic Yogurt, with Oregano Rice and Pan Grilled Broccoli	
Saturday	2 Breakfast Servings 2 Banana Nut Muffins	4 Lunch Servings	2 Servings Poached Salmon with Roasted Garlic Yogurt, with Oregano Rice and Pan Grilled Broccoli	

Week 5 Grocery List

Produce

3 lbs. broccoli
- ◆ 3 white onions
2 lb. zucchini
- ◆ 16 ounces grape or cherry tomatoes
- ◆ 3 shallots
- ◆ 2 red bell peppers
1 ear corn
2 pints fresh strawberries
- ◆ 3 bananas
- ◆ 3 heads garlic
- ◆ 4 Tbsp. fresh lemon juice
1 bunch fresh oregano
1 1/2 lb. sweet potatoes
- ◆ 4 heads romaine lettuce (1 per salad)

Dairy

- ◆ 9 large eggs
- ◆ 3/4 Cup non-fat buttermilk
- ◆ 2 Cups 1% milk
1 Cup 2% milk
- ◆ 1 lb. reduced-fat cheddar cheese
2 1/4 Cups 2% milk
1 ounce goat cheese
1 1/2 Cups non-fat yogurt
1/2 Cup non-fat Greek yogurt
- ◆ 1 1/2 ounce Parmigiano-Reggiano
- ◆ 2 ounces reduced-fat Monterey Jack cheese
- ◆ 3/4 Cup Promise Buttery Spread or Smart Balance Spread

Meat/Fish

8 ounces boneless skinless chicken breast
1 lb. 95% lean ground beef
4 4-ounce salmon filets

Pantry Items

- ◆ 1 Cup Splenda or stevia
1 can canned pumpkin
unsweetened applesauce
- ◆ 1 tsp. pure vanilla extract
molasses
1 1/4 Cup whole wheat flour
1/2 Cup wheat germ
1/4 Cup extra virgin olive oil
3 Cups all purpose white flour
3/4 Cup olive oil
- ◆ 1/2 Cup balsamic vinegar
- ◆ 4 Tbsp. maple syrup
- ◆ 2 Cups quick oats
- ◆ 2 ounces whole wheat fettuccine
- ◆ 8 ounces whole wheat macaroni pasta
- ◆ 2 anchovy filets
- ◆ 2 Tbsp. Dijon mustard
- ◆ 2 Tbsp. honey
- ◆ 1/4 Cup chopped pecans
- ◆ 1/2 tsp. sugar
1 Cup long grain brown rice
1/2 Cup pine nuts
- ◆ 1/2 Cup light brown sugar
2 ounces pepperoncini
low sodium ketchup
- ◆ 4 Tbsp. reduced-fat croutons
- ◆ 4 tsp. salt
- ◆ 3 tsp. baking powder
- ◆ 3/4 tsp. baking soda
- ◆ 1 1/2 tsp. ground cinnamon
- ◆ 2 tsp. ground ginger
- ◆ 2 tsp. dried marjoram
- ◆ 1/4 tsp. paprika
- ◆ 1/2 tsp. dry mustard
- ◆ 1/4 tsp. fresh ground black pepper
- ◆ 1/4 tsp. ground nutmeg
- ◆ 4 tsp. dried sage
1/2 tsp. dried red pepper flakes

Misc.

- ◆ 1/4 Cup white wine
- ◆ 2 Cups mango juice
2 Breakfast Servings
20 Lunch Servings

- ◆ indicates previously purchased - check pantry first

	● Breakfast	▲ Lunch	■ Dinner	To Do
	Week 6 Meal Plan			
Sunday	4 Servings Apple Cinnamon Bread	4 Lunch Servings	2 Servings Shrimp Fried Rice	
Monday	4 Servings Apple Cinnamon Bread	4 Lunch Servings	2 Servings Crab Cakes with Roasted Corn on the Cob and Pan Grilled Asparagus	
Tuesday	4 Servings Healthy Tropical Melon Smoothie	4 Lunch Servings Sandwiches made with leftover Crab Cakes	Eat Out - Fish	
Wednesday	4 Servings Cereal for Breakfast	4 Lunch Servings	2 Servings Stuffed Creole Chicken with Parmesan Squash	Make Blueberry Muffins
Thursday	4 Servings Blueberry Muffins	4 Lunch Servings	2 Servings Lentil Chili	
Friday	2 Breakfast Servings 2 Blueberry Muffins	4 Lunch Servings	2 Servings Lentil Chili	
Saturday	4 Servings Spinach and Feta Frittata	4 Lunch Servings	2 Servings Chicken Leek Risotto	

Week 6 Grocery List

Produce

2 Cups apples
1/2 lb. asparagus
24 ounces cantaloupe
◆ 2 bananas
◆ 1 lb. Yukon gold potatoes
1 lb. zucchini
◆ 4 Tbsp. fresh herbs of your
  choice
4 ounces mushrooms
◆ 2 large shallot
◆ 1 large green bell pepper
◆ 3 ribs celery
◆ 1/2 cup blueberries
◆ 2 cloves garlic
2 large onions
2 small red onions
2 large carrots
4 ounces fresh spinach
2 large leeks
4 servings choice of fruit
2 8-ounce yellow squash
2 ears fresh corn
1 lemon

Dairy

◆ 3 Tbsp. Promise Buttery Spread
or Smart Balance Spread
◆ 1 1/4 Cup non-fat buttermilk
◆ 2 1/2 Cup non-fat yogurt
◆ 18 large eggs
◆ 4 tsp. unsalted butter
◆ 2 1/4 Cup 2% milk
1 ounce reduced fat cream
cheese
◆ 3 ounces Parmigiano-Reggiano
cheese
◆ 3 ounces reduced-fat Monterey
Jack cheese
2 ounces feta cheese
6 Tbsp. non-fat sour cream

Meat/Fish

2 boneless skinless chicken thighs
8 ounces boneless skinless chicken breast
2 4 ounce whitefish filets (trout, cod, drum, or tilapia)
6 ounces shrimp
1 lb. lump crabmeat

Pantry Items (cont.)

1/2 Cup cider vinegar
◆ 1 Cup jasmine rice
◆ 3/4 Cup olive oil
sesame oil
extra-virgin olive oil
◆ 2 tsp. Dijon mustard
◆ 4 Cups cereal of your
  choice (see list)
1 Cup lentils
◆ 1/2 Cup arborio rice
1/2 Cup brown rice
1 15-ounce can no salt added
crushed tomatoes
1/2 chipotle pepper in adobo
sauce (optional)
1 Tbsp. soy sauce
Saltine crackers
Tabasco sauce
Worcestershire sauce
Reduced-fat mayonnaise
◆ 1 tsp. ground cinnamon
◆ salt
◆ 3 tsp. baking powder
◆ 3/4 tsp. baking soda
◆ 2 Tbsp. chili powder
◆ 1/8 tsp. paprika
◆ 1 Tbsp. dried sage
◆ 1 tsp. no salt added Cajun
  or Creole seasoning
◆ 2 tsp. ground cumin
◆ 1 tsp. dried oregano
◆ 1/4 tsp. ground nutmeg
1/8 tsp. dried tarragon
◆ 1/4 tsp. saffron threads

Misc.

◆ 1 1/3 Cup mango or papaya
  juice
2/3 Cup frozen peas

Pantry Items

1/4 Cup pecans
2 tsp. maple syrup
1 1/4 Cup Splenda or Stevia
◆ 1/2 Cup unsweetened apple
  sauce
◆ 1 tsp. pure vanilla extract
◆ 2 1/4 cup all purpose white
flour
◆ 1 1/4 Cup whole wheat flour
◆ 1/2 Cup wheat germ

◆ indicates previously purchased - check pantry first

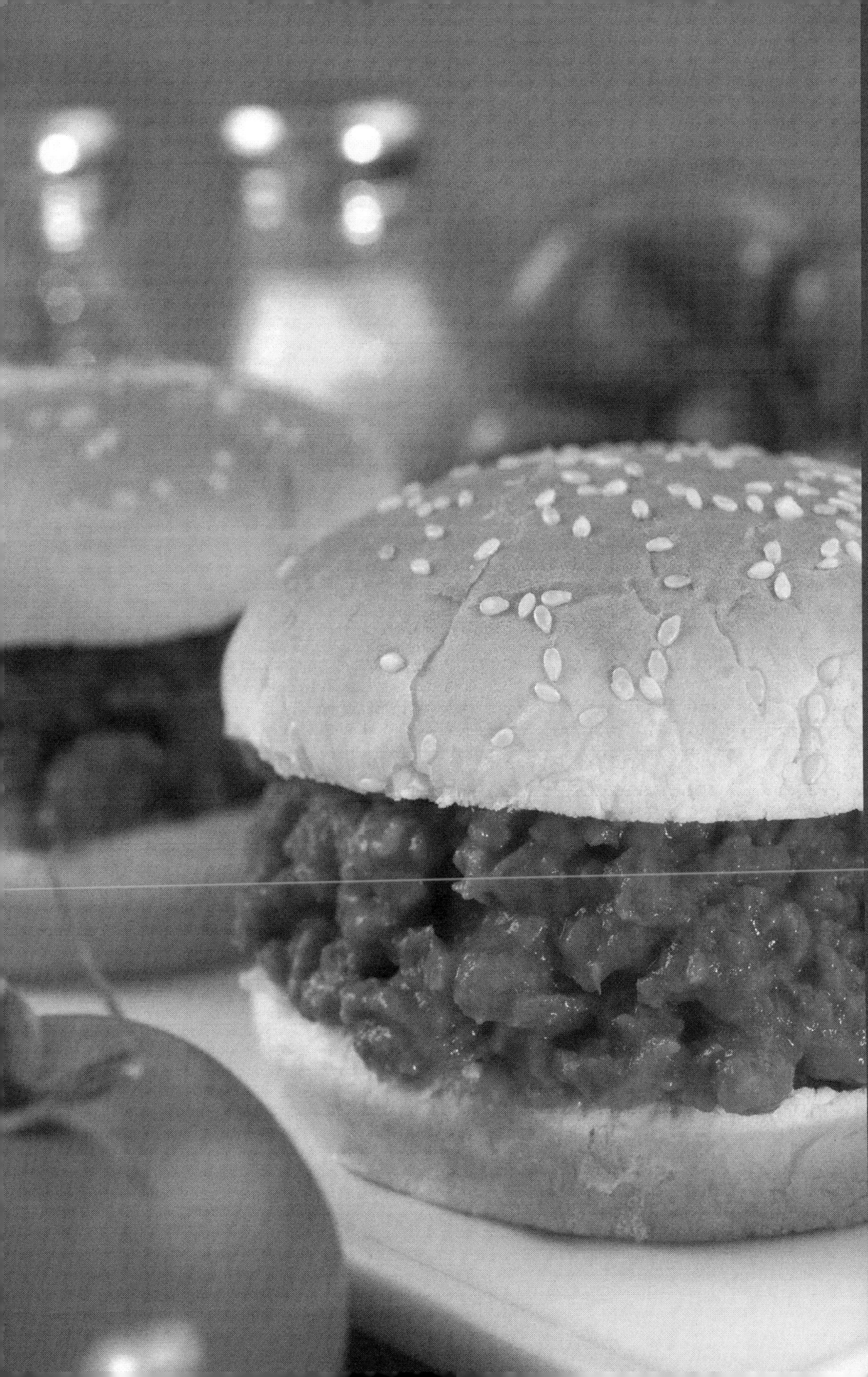

Recipes

Apple Cinnamon Bread

8 **90 min.**

Serving size = 1 slice

This recipe can be multiplied by two but must be cooked in two separate loaf pans. Bread will keep for 72 - 96 hours in a plastic bag. Reheat gently. This will freeze fairly well if sealed tightly in a plastic bag.

1/4 Cup	pecans (coarsely chopped)
2 tsp.	maple syrup
1/4 tsp.	ground cinnamon
1 large	egg yolk
1 Tbsp.	light spread (like Promise But tery Spread Light or Smart Balance Light)
2/3 Cup	Splenda or stevia
1/2 Cup	unsweetened applesauce
1/2 tsp.	pure vanilla extract
3 large	egg whites
1 1/4 Cups	all purpose white flour
3/4 Cup	whole wheat flour
1/4 tsp.	salt
2 tsp.	baking powder
1/2 tsp.	baking soda
1 tsp.	ground cinnamon
1/4 Cup	wheat germ
2 Cups	apples (peeled and diced)
1/2 Cup	non-fat buttermilk

Preheat oven to 350°F. Line a 1 1/2 quart glass Pyrex oblong loaf pan with foil (non-stick foil works best).

Combine a the pecans, maple syrup and cinnamon in a small bowl. Stir until well blended. Set aside.

Whisk the egg yolk until smooth. Add the reduced-fat spread and whisk together until smooth. Add the Splenda®, applesauce and vanilla extract and whisk until smooth.

In separate bowl whisk the egg whites until they begin to be very frothy and white. Do not beat into stiff peaks.

Place the all-purpose flour, whole wheat flour, salt, baking powder, baking soda, cinnamon and wheat germ in a sifter and sift into the mixing bowl.

Gently fold the creamed mixture together with the flour mixture. As this is blended add the grated apples.

Just as the apples are blended in, add the buttermilk and fold until smooth. As soon as the mixture is well blended, add the frothed egg whites and fold together until smooth.

Pour the batter into the lined Pyrex dish. Spread the pecan and maple syrup mixture evenly over the top and place in the preheated oven. Bake for 60 minutes.

"How many apples fell on Newton's head before he took the hint? Nature is always hinting at us. It hints over and over again. And suddenly we take the hint."

Carl Sagan

The refrigerator light goes on...
Making bread is a little more time consuming than a simple muffin recipe, but this Apple Cinnamon quick bread is a great comfort food. Warm and inviting, with a spicy cinnamon aroma, just having this one in the oven makes the house more homey. The loaf will keep well for about 3 - 4 days and it's best to cut two thin slices and toast them lightly in the oven or toaster oven.

Nutrition Facts	
Serving size	1 slice
Servings	8
Calories 193	Calories from Fat 39
	% Daily Value
Total Fat 5 g	7 %
Saturated Fat 1 g	4 %
Trans Fat 0 g	
Monounsaturated Fat 2 g	
Cholesterol 27 mg	9 %
Sodium 312 mg	13 %
Total Carbohydrates 33 g	11 %
Dietary Fiber 3 g	13 %
Sugars 5 g	
Protein 7 g	
Vitamin A 3 %	Vitamin C 7 %
Calcium 9 %	Iron 11 %
Vitamin K 1 mcg	
Potassium 187 mg	
Magnesium 37 mg	

Baked Eggs with Hashbrowns

 2 **30 min.**

Serving size = about 2 cups veggies with 1 egg

This recipe can easily be multiplied but does not make good leftovers.

1 tsp.	olive oil
1 small	onion (diced)
1/2 large	red bell pepper (diced)
12 ounces	sweet potato (large dice)
1/4 tsp.	salt
to taste	fresh ground black pepper
2 tsp.	dried sage
2 large	eggs
1 ounce	reduced-fat Monterey jack cheese (grated)

Preheat the oven to 375° F.

Place the olive oil in a skillet over medium-high heat.

Add the onions and sauté, stirring frequently, for about 2 minutes or until translucent.

Add the bell pepper and continue sautéing for another 2 minutes.

Add the sweet potatoes, stir, and cover. Reduce heat to medium and cook for about 15 minutes, stirring frequently, until the potatoes are soft.

Add the salt, pepper, and sage and stir. Cook for another 5 minutes on low.

Divide the potatoes between two oven proof dishes. Break one egg on top of the potatoes in each dish.

Place the dishes in the oven and bake for about ten minutes until the eggs are almost done to your liking.

Top with the grated cheese and bake for one minute or until the cheese is melted, then serve.

"How often when they find a sage, As sweet as Socrates or Plato; They hand him hemlock for his wage, Or bake him like a sweet potato!"
Don Marquis, Author

The refrigerator light goes on...
I like eggs for dinner. While this is a great dish for a weekend brunch, it makes an equally good choice for a weeknight dinner. The veggies take about 5 minutes to prep and the whole dish is finished easily inside of 30 minutes.

Nutrition Facts	
Serving size	2 cups veggies/1 egg
Servings	2
Calories 369	Calories from Fat 98
	% Daily Value
Total Fat 10 g	17 %
Saturated Fat 4 g	15 %
Trans Fat 0 g	
Monounsaturated Fat 5 g	
Cholesterol 54 mg	19 %
Sodium 465 mg	19 %
Total Carbohydrates 54 g	21 %
Dietary Fiber 9 g	31 %
Sugars 4 g	
Protein 14g	
Vitamin A 33 %	Vitamin C 121 %
Calcium 16 %	Iron 14 %
Vitamin K 19 mcg	
Potassium 1612 mg	
Magnesium 58 mg	

Banana Nut Bread

8 **90 min.**

Serving size = 1 slice

This recipe can easily be multiplied by 2 but must be cooked in separate loaf pans. Bread will keep for 72 - 96 hours in a plastic bag. Reheat gently. This will freeze fairly well if sealed tightly in a plastic bag.

1 large	egg yolk
1 Tbsp.	light spread (like Promise Buttery Spread Light or Smart Balance Light)
2/3 Cup	Splenda or stevia
1/2 tsp.	pure vanilla extract
2 medium	bananas
3 large	egg whites
1 1/4 Cup	all purpose white flour
3/4 Cup	whole wheat flour
1/4 tsp.	salt
2 tsp.	baking powder
1/2 tsp.	baking soda
1/2 tsp.	ground cinnamon
1/4 tsp.	ground nutmeg
1/4 Cup	wheat germ
1/2 Cup	pecans (coarsely chopped)
1/4 Cup	non-fat buttermilk
2 tsp.	light brown sugar

Preheat oven to 350°F. Line a 1 1/2 quart glass Pyrex oblong loaf pan with foil (non-stick foil works best).

Whisk the egg yolk until smooth. Add the reduced-fat spread and whisk together until smooth.

Using the whisk, mash the bananas into the mixture until smooth. Add the Splenda® and vanilla extract and whisk until smooth.

In separate bowl whisk the egg whites until they begin to be very frothy and white. Do not beat into stiff peaks.

Place the all-purpose flour, whole wheat flour, salt, baking powder, baking soda, cinnamon, nutmeg and wheat germ in a sifter and sift into the mixing bowl.

Gently fold the creamed mixture together with the flour mixture. As this is blended add the pecans. As soon as the mixture is well blended add the frothed egg whites and fold together until smooth.

Just as the pecans are blended in, add buttermilk and fold until smooth.

Pour the batter into the lined Pyrex dish and sprinkle the light brown sugar evenly over the top. Place the loaf pan in the preheated oven. Bake for 55 minutes.

"Time flies like an arrow; fruit flies like a banana."
Groucho Marx, Comedian

The refrigerator light goes on...
I love banana nut bread. This healthy recipe has a few more calories than most of the muffins or breads recipes that are on the Dr. Gourmet website, but a lot less fat and sugar than most recipes out there. Even so, a lot of those calories are from monounsaturated fats in the pecans. Best of all? You get 15% of the daily fiber you need.

Nutrition Facts	
Serving size	1 slice
Servings	8
Calories 223	Calories from Fat 60
	% Daily Value
Total Fat 7 g	11 %
Saturated Fat 1 g	4 %
Trans Fat 0 g	
Monounsaturated Fat 3 g	
Cholesterol 27 mg	9 %
Sodium 312 mg	13 %
Total Carbohydrates 35 g	12 %
Dietary Fiber 4 g	15 %
Sugars 6 g	
Protein 7 g	
Vitamin A 3 %	Vitamin C 5 %
Calcium 9 %	Iron 11 %
Vitamin K 1 mcg	
Potassium 271 mg	
Magnesium 48 mg	

Banana Nut Muffins

 6 **30 min.**

Serving size = 1 muffin

This recipe can be multiplied by 2 or 3. They will keep for 24 - 36 hours in a plastic bag, and freeze fairly well if sealed tightly in a plastic bag.

1 large	egg (separated)
2 Tbsp.	light spread (like Promise Buttery Spread Light or Take Control Light)
1 large	banana
1/2 tsp.	pure vanilla extract
1/2 Cup	Splenda or stevia
1/4 Cup	chopped pecans
1 Cup	all purpose white flour
1/2 Cup	whole wheat flour
2 Tbsp.	wheat germ
1/4 tsp.	salt
1 tsp.	baking powder
1/4 tsp.	baking soda
1/2 tsp.	ground cinnamon
1/4 tsp.	ground nutmeg
1/4 Cup	non-fat buttermilk
2 tsp.	light brown sugar

Preheat oven to 375°F.

Using a whisk, cream together the egg yolk and light spread. Add the banana and mash into the mixture until well blended. Add the vanilla extract and Splenda and blend. Fold in the chopped pecans.

Sift the all purpose flour, whole wheat flour, wheat germ, salt, baking powder, baking soda, cinnamon and nutmeg in a sifter and sift into the mixing bowl.

Gently fold the creamed mixture together with the flour mixture until smooth. When blended the mixture will still be dry. Whisk the egg white until it is white and foamy (about tripled in volume). Fold in the egg white.

Fold in the buttermilk, and when the dough is just blended together, stop.

Line a standard size muffin tin with 6 muffin papers and fill each muffin paper with an equal amount of batter. Place the muffins in the oven and bake for 20 minutes.

"The smell of good bread baking, like the sound of lightly flowing water, is indescribable in its evocation of innocence and delight."

M. F. K. Fisher, Author

The refrigerator light goes on...
These muffins can be made with stevia instead of Splenda. Use 12 packets of Truvia brand for each 1/2 cup of Splenda. Z Sweet brand measures like sugar so you will need 1/2 cup of that product.

Nutrition Facts	
Serving size	1 muffin
Servings	6
Calories 208	Calories from Fat 57

	% Daily Value
Total Fat 7 g	10 %
Saturated Fat 1 g	6 %
Trans Fat 0 g	
Monounsaturated Fat 3 g	
Cholesterol 36 mg	12 %
Sodium 282 mg	12 %
Total Carbohydrates 32 g	11 %
Dietary Fiber 3 g	12 %
Sugars 5 g	
Protein 6 g	
Vitamin A 6 %	Vitamin C 4 %
Calcium 7 %	Iron 11 %
Vitamin K 2 mcg	
Potassium 217 mg	
Magnesium 38 mg	

Blueberry Muffins

6 **30 min.**

Serving size = 1 muffin

This recipe can easily be multiplied by 2 or 3. Muffins will keep 24-36 hours in a plastic bag and will freeze fairly well.

2 Tbsp.	light spread (like Promise But tery Spread Light or Smart Balance Light)
1/2 Cup	Splenda or stevia
1 large	egg
2 Tbsp.	non-fat yogurt
1/2 tsp.	pure vanilla extract
1 Cup	all purpose white flour
1/2 Cup	whole wheat flour
2 Tbsp.	wheat germ
1/4 tsp.	salt
1 tsp.	baking powder
1/4 tsp.	baking soda
1/2 Cup	non-fat buttermilk
1/2 Cup	blueberries

Preheat oven to 375°F.

Separate the egg into an egg white and egg yolk. Set the egg yolk aside and whisk the egg white until frothy.

Cream together the reduced-fat spread and egg yolk until smooth. Add the Splenda®, yogurt and vanilla extract.

Whisk until smooth.

Place the all-purpose flour, whole wheat flour, wheat germ, salt, baking powder and baking soda in a sifter and sift into the mixing bowl.

Gently fold the creamed mixture together with the flour mixture. As this is blended slowly add the buttermilk folding until smooth. As soon as the mixture is well blended, stop.

Froth the egg whites until white and foamy and fold them into the batter. Gently fold the blueberries into the batter. Do not over mix.

Line a muffin tin with muffin papers and fill each muffin paper with an equal amount of batter. Bake for 12 – 15 minutes.

"Some people like cupcakes better. I, for one, care less for them!"

Frank Zappa, Musician

The refrigerator light goes on...
This is a great, healthy muffin that's so much better for you than a regular muffin. When I started with Dr. Gourmet I wanted to make food that people found familiar but healthier. This takes that a step further than the previous Blueberry Muffins posted on the website because of the higher fiber content. One taster said that these "are so much better tasting than the original." That's what great food is – good food that just happens to be better for you.

Nutrition Facts	
Serving size	1 muffin
Servings	6
Calories 181	Calories from Fat 42
	% Daily Value
Total Fat 5 g	7 %
Saturated Fat 1 g	7 %
Trans Fat 0 g	
Monounsaturated Fat 2 g	
Cholesterol 36 mg	12 %
Sodium 296 mg	12 %
Total Carbohydrates 29 g	10 %
Dietary Fiber 2 g	10 %
Sugars 4 g	
Protein 6 g	
Vitamin A 5 %	Vitamin C 2 %
Calcium 9 %	Iron 10 %
Vitamin K 5 mcg	
Potassium 152 mg	
Magnesium 29 mg	

Blueberry Pancakes

 30 min.

Serving size = 2 pancakes, with 2 tsp. light spread and 1 Tbsp. pure maple syrup

This recipe can easily be multiplied, but leftover pancakes aren't very good. The batter will keep overnight, but the pancakes will not be as good.

2/3 Cup	all purpose white flour
1 Tbsp.	Splenda or stevia
1 tsp.	baking powder
2/3 Cup	non-fat buttermilk
1/4 Cup	egg substitute
1 tsp.	pure vanilla extract
1/4 Cup	fresh blueberries (or strawberries or blackberries)
2 tsp. per serving	Take Control Spread Light (or Promise Buttery Spread Light)
1 Tbsp. per serving	pure maple syrup

Sift flour, Splenda and baking powder into a large mixing bowl.

Add buttermilk, egg substitute and vanilla extract and blend using a large whisk until smooth.

Heat a non-stick griddle over medium-high heat. Let the batter stand for at least 2 minutes while the griddle is heating. Stir once and wait another minute before placing batter on the griddle.

When the griddle is hot enough that a few drops of water will dance on the surface, reduce the heat to medium and place about 1/4 cup of batter for each pancake on the griddle.

After the pancakes have cooked for about a minute spread a tablespoon of fruit across the top of each one. Allow to cook for another 1 - 2 minutes until bubbles form on the surface and burst. Turn pancake and cook for about 1/2 the time of the first side until the are golden brown.

Remove and top with one teaspoon of Promise Buttery Spread Light on each pancake and serve one tablespoon of pure maple syrup for every two pancakes.

"Aspiring to a soufflé, he achieves a pancake at which the reader saws without much appetite."
John Leonard, Author

The refrigerator light goes on...
I love adding fruit to my pancakes. Any berry will do – blueberries, strawberries, blackberries – whatever is in the market. I have not had much success using frozen berries in my pancakes, however.

Nutrition Facts	
Serving size	2 pancakes
Servings	2
Calories 294	Calories from Fat 49
	% Daily Value
Total Fat 6 g	9 %
Saturated Fat 1 g	7 %
Trans Fat 0 g	
Monounsaturated Fat 2 g	
Cholesterol 2 mg	1 %
Sodium 404 mg	17 %
Total Carbohydrates 50 g	17 %
Dietary Fiber 5 g	19 %
Sugars 14 g	
Protein 12 g	
Vitamin A 15 %	Vitamin C 4 %
Calcium 29 %	Iron 15 %
Vitamin K 7 mcg	
Potassium 468 mg	
Magnesium 75 mg	

Creole Frittata

 2 **30 min.**

Serving Size = 1/2 pie

This recipe can be multiplied by 2 but will require a larger skillet. Leftovers are good. Wrap tightly after cooled and refrigerate. I like to make sandwiches from left over frittata.

	spray olive oil
1/2 medium	onion (diced)
2 large	eggs
2 large	egg whites
2 tsp.	water
to taste	fresh ground black pepper
1 tsp.	no salt added Creole or Cajun seasoning blend
2 ounces	reduced fat cheddar cheese (shredded)

Preheat the oven to 425°F.

Place a small non-stick sauté pan over medium-high heat and spray lightly with olive oil. Add the diced onion and cook slowly until translucent and soft. It is fine if the onions brown and caramelize.

Whisk the eggs, egg whites, water, pepper and Creole seasoning in a bowl until frothy.

Add the egg mixture to the onions and stir well. Reduce the heat to medium. Simmer for about 2 minutes.

Spread the shredded cheddar cheese over the top of the onions and place the pan in the oven.

Cook for about 12 minutes until the frittata is puffed and slightly firm to the touch.

"I have met a lot of hardboiled eggs in my time, but you're twenty minutes."

Oscar Wilde, Poet

The refrigerator light goes on...

Frittatas make an easy and elegant alternative to the ordinary breakfast and they only take a few minutes to make. You don't have to use the oven (if it's summer and you don't want to heat up the kitchen, for instance). Simply reduce the heat on the range to very low and put a cover over the pan. You'll want to remove the lid about every 3 - 4 minutes or so to let the steam escape.

When choosing Creole seasoning make sure to choose not only one labeled "no salt added" but also check to see that salt substitute is not an ingredient. Often potassium chloride is used and will give a salty metallic taste to your dishes.

I have used three excellent brands including Paul Prudhomme, McCormick and Spice Hunter. They are sodium and potassium free – just spice.

Nutrition Facts	
Serving size	1/2 pie
Servings	2
Calories 162	Calories from Fat 69
	% Daily Value
Total Fat 8 g	12 %
Saturated Fat 3 g	15 %
Trans Fat 0 g	
Monounsaturated Fat 3 g	
Cholesterol 243 mg	81 %
Sodium 310 mg	13 %
Total Carbohydrates 5 g	2 %
Dietary Fiber 1 g	4 %
Sugars 3 g	
Protein 18 g	
Vitamin A 12 %	Vitamin C 6 %
Calcium 16 %	Iron 8 %
Vitamin K 2 mcg	
Potassium 220 mg	
Magnesium 20 mg	

Gingerbread

 8 **60 min.**

Serving size = 1 slice

This recipe can be multiplied by 2 but you will need 2 loaf pans. Bread will keep for 72 - 96 hours in a plastic bag. Reheat gently. This will freeze fairly well if sealed tightly in a plastic bag.

1 large	egg yolk
1 Tbsp.	light spread (like Promise Buttery Spread Light or Smart Balance Light)
1/2 Cup	Splenda or stevia
1/2 Cup	canned pumpkin
1/2 Cup	unsweetened applesauce
1/2 tsp.	pure vanilla extract
2 Tbsp.	molasses
3 large.	egg whites
1 1/4 Cup	all purpose flour
3/4 Cup	whole wheat flour
1/4 tsp.	salt
2 tsp.	baking powder
1/2 tsp.	baking soda
1 tsp.	ground cinnamon
2 tsp.	ground ginger
1/4 Cup	wheat germ
1/2 Cup	non-fat buttermilk

Preheat oven to 350°F. Line a 1 1/2 quart glass Pyrex oblong loaf pan with foil (non-stick foil works best).

Whisk the egg yolk until smooth. Add the reduced-fat spread and whisk together until smooth. Add the Splenda®, applesauce, pumpkin and vanilla extract and whisk until smooth. Whisk in the molasses.

In separate bowl whisk the egg whites until they begin to be very frothy and white. Do not beat into stiff peaks (the egg whites should about triple in volume).

Place the all-purpose flour, whole wheat flour, salt, baking powder, baking soda, cinnamon, ginger and wheat germ in a sifter and sift into the mixing bowl.

Gently fold the creamed mixture together with the flour mixture. Add buttermilk and fold until smooth. As soon as the mixture is well blended add the frothed egg whites and fold together until smooth.

Pour the batter into the lined Pyrex dish. Place the loaf pan in the preheated oven. Bake for 50 minutes.

"You have to eat oatmeal or you'll dry up. Anybody knows that."

> Eloise, Star of Kay
> Thompson's Eloise books

The refrigerator light goes on...
This is such an easy recipe to make and gingerbread is the perfect breakfast. Low in calories and fat and high in fiber, you can't go wrong with the flavors that you loved as a kid.

Nutrition Facts	
Serving size	1 slice
Servings	8
Calories 168	Calories from Fat 18

	% Daily Value
Total Fat 2 g	3 %
Saturated Fat 1 g	3 %
Trans Fat 0 g	
Monounsaturated Fat 1 g	
Cholesterol 27 mg	9 %
Sodium 283 mg	12 %
Total Carbohydrates 32 g	11 %
Dietary Fiber 3 g	11 %
Sugars 4 g	
Protein 6 g	
Vitamin A 50 %	Vitamin C 7 %
Calcium 11 %	Iron 12 %
Vitamin K 3 mcg	
Potassium 245 mg	
Magnesium 44 mg	

Healthy Strawberry Banana Smoothie

 1 **15 min.**

Serving size = 1 smoothie: about 1 1/2 cups

This recipe can easily be multiplied but does not keep well.

1/4 Cup	non-fat yogurt
1 Cup	fresh strawberries
1/2 Cup	mango juice
1/2	banana

Place the yogurt, strawberries, mango juice and banana in a blender and blend on high until smooth.

"Sure I eat what I advertise. Sure I eat Wheaties for breakfast. A good bowl of Wheaties with bourbon can't be beat."

Dizzy Dean, Baseball Player

The refrigerator light goes on...
A smoothie can make a great breakfast if you're on the run and only have a few seconds. Use a base of non-fat yogurt for a good protein source and a lot of fruit for good carbs and fiber. I like using papaya or mango juice because they gives a good thick texture and are easy on the stomach.

Nutrition Facts	
Serving size	1 smoothie
Servings	1
Calories 234	Calories from Fat 0
	% Daily Value
Total Fat 1 g	1 %
Saturated Fat 0 g	1 %
Trans Fat 0 g	
Monounsaturated Fat 0 g	
Cholesterol 32 mg	1 %
Sodium 103 mg	4 %
Total Carbohydrates 51 g	17 %
Dietary Fiber 5 g	20 %
Sugars 40 g	
Protein 9 g	
Vitamin A 19 %	Vitamin C 191 %
Calcium 29 %	Iron 7 %
Vitamin K 5 mcg	
Potassium 786 mg	
Magnesium 63 mg	

Healthy Toasted Oatmeal

 15 min.

Serving size = about 1 cup

This recipe can easily be multiplied but does not make good leftovers.

1/2 Cup	quick oats
1/2 Cup	water
1/2 Cup	2% milk
1/16 tsp.	salt
1 1/2 tsp.	light brown sugar
1 tsp.	light spread (like Promise Buttery Spread Light or Smart Balance Light)

Place a medium sized stainless steel skillet over medium-high heat. Add the oatmeal and cook the about 5 minutes, stirring very frequently.

The little bits of oatmeal can burn if you're not careful, so it's important to stir frequently. Reduce the heat to medium if it looks like it's cooking too fast. When it smells a little like cooked popcorn it is ready. The oatmeal will be a golden brown about the color of toast.

Remove the pan from the heat and add the water. The water will boil up, and as it settles down to a simmer, put the pan over low-medium heat. Add the milk, salt and sugar.

Cook for about five more minutes and swirl the pan frequently. The oatmeal is done when nearly all of the liquid has cooked away. At that point add the teaspoon of light spread and stir until it melts. Serve.

"Trying a case the second time is like eating yesterday morning's oatmeal."
Lloyd Paul Stryker, Attorney

The refrigerator light goes on...
This recipe was submitted by a reader and the minute I saw it I was taken in. I love toasting my nuts before I use them because it really brings out their flavor. I thought that oatmeal would be the same and it is. This is really fantastic. It takes all of ten minutes to make. Come on, you've got ten minutes. You'll stand in line that long at whatever fast food place you might go to.

Nutrition Facts	
Serving size	about 1 cup
Servings	1
Calories 265	Calories from Fat 58

	% Daily Value
Total Fat 7 g	10 %
Saturated Fat 2 g	12 %
Trans Fat 0 g	
Monounsaturated Fat 2 g	
Cholesterol 10 mg	3 %
Sodium 246 mg	10 %
Total Carbohydrates 40 g	13 %
Dietary Fiber 4 g	16 %
Sugars 14 g	
Protein 11 g	
Vitamin A 5 %	Vitamin C 2 %
Calcium 20 %	Iron 11 %
Vitamin K 3 mcg	
Potassium 82 mg	
Magnesium 390 mg	

Healthy Tropical Melon Smoothie

 15 min.

Serving size = 1 smoothie: about 1 1/2 cups

This recipe can easily be multiplied but does not keep well.

1/2 Cup	non-fat yogurt
6 ounces	cantaloupe
1/2	banana
1/3 Cup	mango or papaya juice

Place the yogurt, melon, banana and papaya juice in a blender and blend on high until smooth.

"Sometimes I've believed as many as six impossible things before breakfast."
Lewis Carroll, Writer

The refrigerator light goes on...
A smoothie can make a great breakfast if you're on the run and only have a few seconds. Use a base of non-fat yogurt for a good protein source and a lot of fruit for good carbs and fiber. I like using papaya or mango juice because they give a good thick texture and are easy on the stomach.

Nutrition Facts	
Serving size	about 1 1/2 cups
Servings	1
Calories 215	Calories from Fat 6
	% Daily Value
Total Fat 1 g	1 %
Saturated Fat 0 g	1 %
Trans Fat 0 g	
Monounsaturated Fat 0 g	
Cholesterol 3 mg	1 %
Sodium 115 mg	5 %
Total Carbohydrates 47 g	16 %
Dietary Fiber 3 g	11 %
Sugars 39 g	
Protein 9 g	
Vitamin A 78 %	Vitamin C 96 %
Calcium 28 %	Iron 5 %
Vitamin K 4 mcg	
Potassium 790 mg	
Magnesium 54 mg	

Omelet

2 **15 min.**

Serving size = 1/2 omelet

This recipe can easily be multiplied by 2 or more but must be cooked in a larger skillet. I do occasionally keep the other half of an omelet and make sandwiches with it.

1/2 tsp.	unsalted butter
1/6	green bell pepper (julienne strips)
2 large	egg whites
1 large	egg yolk
1 1/2 Tbsp.	water
3 large	fresh basil leaves
to taste	fresh ground black pepper
1/4 ounce	Parmigiano-Reggiano (grated)

Melt the butter in a small non-stick skillet pan over medium heat. Add the peppers and cook until they are browned but not limp. Remove and set aside.

In a small mixing bowl whisk together the egg whites, eggs yolks and water. Add ground pepper to taste.

Heat a medium sized non-stick skillet over medium-high heat and place the basil in the bottom and pour the egg mixture over the top. Reduce the heat to medium heat and cook slowly. Gently slide a spatula under the eggs and carefully fold back the cooked portion so as to expose more uncooked egg to the bottom of the pan.

When the eggs are nearly set, add the peppers to the center (in a straight line so as to make folding easier). Fold the omelet in half over the peppers. Cook about 2 more minutes and remove.

Sprinkle the Parmigiano-Reggiano over the top of the omelet and then divide into two portions.

"My wife and I tried to breakfast together, but we had to stop or our marriage would have been wrecked."

Winston Churchill, British Statesman

The refrigerator light goes on...
Be adventurous with your omelet. Substitute different veggies, herbs and even cheese. Try mushrooms with a bit of cilantro, a pinch of cumin and reduced fat Monterey jack cheese. Making an omelet takes all of 15 minutes in the morning. That's how long you'll wait in line at a fast food joint.

Nutrition Facts	
Serving size	1/2 omelet
Servings	2
Calories 144	Calories from Fat 77
	% Daily Value
Total Fat 9 g	13 %
Saturated Fat 4 g	20 %
Trans Fat 0 g	
Monounsaturated Fat 3 g	
Cholesterol 220 mg	73 %
Sodium 232 mg	10 %
Total Carbohydrates 3 g	1 %
Dietary Fiber 1 g	4 %
Sugars 1 g	
Protein 13 g	
Vitamin A 29 %	Vitamin C 32 %
Calcium 14 %	Iron 7 %
Vitamin K 7 mcg	
Potassium 260 mg	
Magnesium 29 mg	

Pecan Peach Muffins

 6   **30 min.**

Serving size = 1 muffin

This recipe can be multiplied by 2 or 3. Muffins will keep for 24 - 36 hours in a plastic bag. These freeze fairly well if sealed tightly in a plastic bag.

1 large	egg, separated
2 Tbsp.	light spread (like Promise Buttery Spread Light or Smart Balance Light)
8 ounces	frozen peaches (thawed and mashed)
1/2 tsp.	pure vanilla extract
1/2 Cup	Splenda or stevia
2 Tbsp.	honey
1 Cup	all purpose flour
1/2 Cup	whole wheat flour
2 Tbsp.	wheat germ
1/4 tsp.	salt
1 tsp.	baking powder
1/4 tsp.	baking soda
1/2 tsp.	ground nutmeg
2 Tbsp.	non-fat buttermilk
2 tsp.	light brown sugar
1/4 Cup	chopped pecans

Using a whisk, cream together the egg yolk and light spread. Add the peaches and mash into the mixture until well blended. Add the vanilla extract, Splenda and honey. Blend well.

Sift the all purpose flour, whole wheat flour, wheat germ, salt, baking powder, baking soda and nutmeg in a sifter and sift into the mixing bowl.

Gently fold the creamed mixture together with the flour mixture until smooth. When blended the mixture will still be dry. Whisk the egg white until it is white and foamy (about tripled in volume). Fold in the egg white.

Fold in the buttermilk and when the dough is just blended together, stop.

Line a standard size muffin tin with 6 muffin papers

and fill each muffin paper with an equal amount of batter.

Mix together the brown sugar and pecans and then sprinkle over the top of the muffins. Place the muffins in the oven and bake for 20 - 25 minutes.

"Chocolate's okay, but I prefer a really intense fruit taste. You know when a peach is absolutely perfect... it's sublime. I'd like to capture that and then use it in a dessert."
Kathy Mattea, Singer

The refrigerator light goes on...
This is a light and lovely muffin perfumed with peach and honey and nutmeg. Perfect summer aromas and flavors any time of year.

Nutrition Facts	
Serving size	1 muffin
Servings	6
Calories 214	Calories from Fat 55
	% Daily Value
Total Fat 6 g	10 %
Saturated Fat 1 g	6 %
Trans Fat 0 g	
Monounsaturated Fat 3 g	
Cholesterol 35 mg	12 %
Sodium 276 mg	12 %
Total Carbohydrates 35 g	12 %
Dietary Fiber 3 g	11 %
Sugars 11 g	
Protein 6 g	
Vitamin A 8 %	Vitamin C 4 %
Calcium 7 %	Iron 10 %
Vitamin K 3 mcg	
Potassium 182 mg	
Magnesium 30 mg	

Pecan Sweet Potato Bread

8 · **60 min.**

Serving size = 1 slice

This recipe can be multiplied by 2 but must be cooked in separate loaf pans. Bread will keep for 72 - 96 hours in a plastic bag. Reheat gently. This will freeze fairly well if sealed tightly in a plastic bag.

1	8 ounce yam (peeled and diced)
1 large	egg yolk
1 Tbsp.	light spread (like Promise Buttery Spread Light or Smart Balance Light)
1/2 Cup	Splenda or stevia
1 tsp.	pure vanilla extract
1/2 Cup	chopped pecans
3 large	egg whites
1 1/4 Cup	all purpose flour
3/4 Cup	whole wheat flour
1/4 tsp.	salt
2 tsp.	baking powder
1/2 tsp.	baking soda
1/2 tsp.	ground cinnamon
2 Tbsp.	wheat germ
1/4 Cup	non-fat buttermilk
2 tsp.	light brown sugar

Steam the yams until they are tender. Mash them with a fork or whisk. Don't try to make the yams into a puree but there should be some small pieces.

Preheat oven to 350°F. Line a 1 1/2 quart glass Pyrex oblong loaf pan with foil (non-stick foil works best).

Whisk the egg yolk until smooth. Add the reduced-fat spread and whisk together until smooth. Add the Splenda®, mashed yams and vanilla extract and whisk. Fold in the chopped pecans.

In separate bowl whisk the egg whites until they begin to be very frothy and white. Do not beat into stiff peaks (the egg whites should about triple in volume).

Place the all-purpose flour, whole wheat flour, salt, baking powder, baking soda, cinnamon and wheat germ in a sifter and sift into the mixing bowl.

Gently fold the creamed mixture together with the flour mixture. Add buttermilk and fold until smooth. As soon as the mixture is well blended add the frothed egg whites and fold together until smooth.

Pour the batter into the lined Pyrex dish. Sprinkle the brown sugar over the top of the bread and place the loaf pan in the preheated oven. Bake for 50 minutes.

"The smell of good bread baking, like the sound of lightly flowing water, is indescribable in its evocation of innocence and delight."

M. F. K. Fisher, Author

The refrigerator light goes on...
This is a denser bread that is subtly sweet. Unlike many baked goods it doesn't have a dominant flavor but a subtle combination of the sweet potato, nuts and spice. Great toasted with a touch of jam or even a bit of light cream cheese.

Nutrition Facts	
Serving size	1 slice
Servings	8
Calories 224	Calories from Fat 58
	% Daily Value
Total Fat 7 g	10 %
Saturated Fat 1 g	5 %
Trans Fat 0 g	
Monounsaturated Fat 3 g	
Cholesterol 27 mg	9 %
Sodium 275 mg	11 %
Total Carbohydrates 35 g	12 %
Dietary Fiber 4 g	16 %
Sugars 2 g	
Protein 7 g	
Vitamin A 3 %	Vitamin C 8 %
Calcium 10 %	Iron 11 %
Vitamin K 2 mcg	
Potassium 378 mg	
Magnesium 41 mg	

Spinach and Feta Frittata

 2 **30 min.**

Serving size = 1/2 frittata

This recipe can easily be multiplied. This recipe makes good leftovers, especially as sandwiches.

1 tsp.	olive oil
1 small	red onion (thinly sliced)
3 large	eggs
2 large	egg whites
2 Tbsp.	water
1/8 tsp.	salt
to taste	fresh ground black pepper
1/8 tsp.	ground nutmeg
1 Tbsp.	Parmigiano-Reggiano (grated)
2 ounces	fresh spinach (coarsely chopped)
1 ounce	feta cheese (crumbled)

Preheat the oven to 325°F. Place the olive oil in a medium oven proof skillet over medium high heat. Add the onion and cook for about 5 minutes until lightly browned.

Whisk together the eggs, egg whites, water, salt, pepper, nutmeg, parmesan and spinach.

Pour the egg mixture into the pan with the onions. Stir and cook for about 1 minute.

Sprinkle the crumbled feta cheese over the top and place the pan into the oven.

Cook for about 15 minutes until the frittata is firm.

"Although I cannot lay an egg, I am a very good judge of omelettes."
George Bernard Shaw, Playwright

The refrigerator light goes on...
Frittatas make the perfect weekend brunch and they're great when you have guests. You can serve them hot fresh out of the oven, but they're great cold as well.

Nutrition Facts	
Serving size	1/2 frittata
Servings	2
Calories 209	Calories from Fat 117
	% Daily Value
Total Fat 13 g	20 %
Saturated Fat 5 g	25 %
Trans Fat 0 g	
Monounsaturated Fat 5 g	
Cholesterol 330 mg	110 %
Sodium 499 mg	21 %
Total Carbohydrates 7 g	2 %
Dietary Fiber 1 g	6 %
Sugars 4 g	
Protein 17 g	
Vitamin A 61 %	Vitamin C 19 %
Calcium 16 %	Iron 13 %
Vitamin K 137 mcg	
Potassium 392 mg	
Magnesium 43 mg	

Yam and Leek Tortilla

2 **30 min.**

Serving size = 1/2 tortilla

This recipe can easily be multiplied but requires multiple skillets. This recipe makes good leftovers served cold or in sandwiches.

1 tsp.	olive oil
1 large	leek (cleaned and sliced crosswise)
8 ounces	yams (peeled and cut into 1/4 inch cubes)
1/4 tsp.	salt
to taste	fresh ground black pepper
1/4 tsp.	dried thyme leaves
1/4 tsp.	dried oregano
2 large	egg whites
2 large	eggs
1 Tbsp.	water

Preheat the oven to 325°F.

Place a medium skillet over medium high heat.

When the pan is hot add the oil and the leeks. Cook for about 5 minutes, stirring frequently.

Add the diced yams and cook for about two minutes. Stir and cover. Reduce the heat to medium and cook for about 12 – 15 minutes, tossing frequently.

Add the salt, pepper, thyme and oregano. Toss well.

Whisk the eggs, egg whites and water together until fluffy. Pour over the top of the leek and yams and then place the pan in the oven.

Cook for about 10 to 12 minutes, or until the egg is set.

Serve.

"To eat well in England you should have breakfast three times a day."
W. Somerset Maugham, Author

The refrigerator light goes on...
I love the yams diced and cooked with the leek like home fries and then made into a tortilla. It's really delicious and a complete breakfast.

Nutrition Facts	
Serving size	1/2 tortilla
Servings	2
Calories 328	Calories from Fat 72
	% Daily Value
Total Fat 7 g	12 %
Saturated Fat 2 g	7 %
Trans Fat 0 g	
Monounsaturated Fat 4 g	
Cholesterol 212 mg	71 %
Sodium 454 mg	17 %
Total Carbohydrates 52 g	17 %
Dietary Fiber 8 g	26 %
Sugars 7 g	
Protein 14 g	
Vitamin A 54 %	Vitamin C 62 %
Calcium 13 %	Iron 25 %
Vitamin K 74 mcg	
Potassium 1304 mg	
Magnesium 74 mg	

Bok Choy Slaw

Servings = 2
Serving size = about 1 cup

This recipe can easily be multiplied and keeps well for about 48 hours in the refrigerator.

8 ounces	bok choy (thinly sliced)
1/4 Cup	fresh basil leaves (chiffonade)
2 tsp.	dark sesame oil
1 tsp.	rice vinegar
2 tsp.	low sodium soy sauce
1/2 tsp.	sugar
to taste	fresh ground black pepper
1 tsp.	white or black sesame seeds

Place the bok choy, basil, sesame oil, rice vinegar, soy sauce, sugar and pepper in a stainless or glass mixing bowl. Toss well and chill.

"Idealist: One who, on noticing that a rose smells better than a cabbage, concludes that it will also make better soup."

H. L. Mencken, Journalist

The refrigerator light goes on...
This is a simple recipe but oh so flavorful. It will go with almost any Asian style meal that you choose as a side dish. It is a little better if you can find spicy Thai basil (which always seems to grow better in my garden than sweet basil). I prefer to use the large bok choy for this salad rather than the little baby bok choy. The texture is a little more coarse and the leaves slightly more bitter but I feel that it makes a better salad. You can also use thinly sliced napa cabbage for this salad.

Nutrition Facts	
Serving size	about 1 cup
Servings	2
Calories 51	Calories from Fat 28
	% Daily Value
Total Fat 3 g	5 %
Saturated Fat 0.5 g	2 %
Trans Fat 0 g	
Monounsaturated Fat 1 g	
Cholesterol 0 mg	0 %
Sodium 248 mg	10 %
Total Carbohydrates 4 g	1 %
Dietary Fiber 1 g	6 %
Sugars 2 g	
Protein 2 g	
Vitamin A 103 %	Vitamin C 85 %
Calcium 14 %	Iron 7 %
Vitamin K 64 mcg	
Potassium 309 mg	
Magnesium 30 mg	

Caesar Salad

Serving size = 1 small salad

This recipe can easily be multiplied. The dressing keeps well tightly sealed in the refrigerator for 5-7 days.

2 cloves	garlic (minced)
2	anchovy filets
1/4 tsp.	fresh ground black pepper
2 Tbsp.	fresh lemon juice
2 Tbsp.	Dijon mustard
2 Tbsp.	honey
1 1/2 ounces	Parmigiano-Reggiano (grated)
1/2 Cup	non-fat yogurt
8	heads romaine lettuce (1 per salad) (sliced crosswise)
1 cup	reduced-fat croutons

Place the garlic, anchovies, pepper, lemon juice, mustard, honey, parmesan cheese and yogurt in a blender and process until smooth.

Chill for at least 2 hours.

Each salad requires 1 head of Romaine lettuce. Rinse the lettuce, drain and pat dry with a paper towel (or use a salad spinner). Cut crosswise and place in refrigerator until needed.

Toss together with the romaine lettuce and croutons. Serve.

"I came, I saw, I conquered."
Julius Caesar

The refrigerator light goes on...
This recipe is rich, creamy and tastes like any Caesar Salad because it has all the elements that your mouth expects. I will say this over and over – the best ingredients make great food.

Nutrition Facts	
Serving size	1 small salad
Servings	8
Calories 94	Calories from Fat 20
	% Daily Value
Total Fat 2 g	4 %
Saturated Fat 1 g	5 %
Trans Fat 0 g	
Monounsaturated Fat 1 g	
Cholesterol 5 mg	2 %
Sodium 219 mg	9 %
Total Carbohydrates 14 g	5 %
Dietary Fiber 4 g	15 %
Sugars 8 g	
Protein 6 g	
Vitamin A 182 %	Vitamin C 67 %
Calcium 16 %	Iron 10 %
Vitamin K 161 mcg	
Potassium 457 mg	
Magnesium 31 mg	

Chicken and Basil Salad

 30 min.

Serving size = 4 ounces salad

This recipe can easily be multiplied and keeps well for 2 – 3 days in the refrigerator.

3	fresh limes (juiced)
4 Tbsp.	shallots (minced)
3 cloves	garlic (minced)
1/4 tsp.	salt
2 Tbsp.	extra virgin olive oil
1 Tbsp.	honey
4 Cups	water
1 Cup	white wine
4	4-ounce boneless, skinless chicken breasts
1/2 Cup	fresh basil (chopped)

Combine lime juice, shallots, garlic, salt, olive oil and honey in a large mixing bowl and chill well.

Place water and wine in a shallow pan over high heat. When the liquid is at a shiver reduce the heat to medium so that it won't boil. Add the chicken breasts and poach until just done. This should take about 10 minutes; check for an internal temperature of 170° to ensure that the meat is cooked.

When the chicken is cooked through, remove it to a cutting board and cut into strips about 1/4 to 1/2 inch wide and 3 to 4 inches long.

While chicken is still warm, add to the chilled lime mixture and toss to coat well.

Add the basil and toss to coat.

Chill at least 6 hours.

"The Bluebird of Happiness long absent from his life, Ned is visited by the Chicken of Depression."
Gary Larson, Cartoonist

The refrigerator light goes on...
Using a little honey in a vinaigrette will help reduce the total fat content and take some of the tart edge off of the acidity of the lime. Keep in mind that there are still a lot of calories in honey.

I don't feel that this salad works as well with dried basil. The flavor is not fresh and bright. If there's no quality fresh basil available, I would make another dish.

Nutrition Facts	
Serving size	4 ounces salad
Servings	4
Calories 268	Calories from Fat 21
	% Daily Value
Total Fat 8 g	13 %
Saturated Fat 1 g	7 %
Trans Fat 0 g	
Monounsaturated Fat 5 g	
Cholesterol 66 mg	22 %
Sodium 225 mg	9 %
Total Carbohydrates 11 g	4 %
Dietary Fiber 0 g	0 %
Sugars 5 g	
Protein 27 g	
Vitamin A 9 %	Vitamin C 20 %
Calcium 4 %	Iron 8 %
Vitamin K 26 mcg	
Potassium 432 mg	
Magnesium 47 mg	

Chinese Chicken Salad

4 **45 min.**

Serving size = about 3 Cups

This recipe can easily be multiplied by 2 and keeps well overnight.

3 quarts	water
8 ounces	whole wheat udon noodles
2 tsp.	dark sesame oil
4 ounces	shiitake mushrooms (thinly sliced)
	spray oil
1/4 Cup	slivered almonds
16 ounces	boneless skinless chicken breast
1 Tbsp.	low-sodium soy sauce
8 ounces	napa cabbage (thinly sliced)
8 ounces	carrots (peeled and thinly sliced)
4 ounces	snow peas
3 Tbsp.	hoisin sauce
2 Tbsp.	rice vinegar
2 Tbsp.	pineapple juice
1	11-ounce can mandarin oranges (drained)
2 tsp.	black sesame seeds (optional)

Place the water in a medium stock pot over high heat.

When water boils, add the udon noodles and cook for 6-8 minutes. Drain, shaking off excess water, then place in a large mixing bowl. Add sesame oil, toss until coated, then place in refrigerator.

While the water is coming to a boil, place a large non-stick skillet over medium-high heat. Spray lightly with oil and add sliced mushrooms. Cook mushrooms, tossing frequently, until they begin to brown. Add almonds and continue cooking until almonds are lightly browned. Remove from heat and set aside.

Preheat oven to 375 and place a large skillet in the oven. When preheated, spray the pan lightly with oil and add the chicken breasts. Cook for 8 minutes, then turn the chicken. Add soy sauce and cook for an additional 5-7 minutes, or until chicken is cooked through.

Once cooked, remove chicken from the oven and cut into 1/4 inch strips. Chill.

While the chicken is cooking, whisk together hoisin sauce, rice vinegar, and pineapple juice in a small bowl. Chill.

When the chicken is cool fold together with the udon noodles, napa cabbage, carrots, snow peas and dressing. Serve topped with the mushroom and almond mixture and the mandarin oranges. Garnish with sesame seeds.

"Chicken salad has a certain glamour about it. Like the little black dress, it is chic and adaptable anywhere."

Laurie Colwin, Author

The refrigerator light goes on...
Light and filling, this has everything you want in a salad - fresh crunchy veggies, a sweet & sour dressing, savory meat.... You can make everything ahead and assemble at the last minute. If you can't find udon noodles in your grocery, use whole wheat linguine.

Nutrition Facts	
Serving size	about 3 cups
Servings	4
Calories 551	Calories from Fat 82
	% Daily Value
Total Fat 9 g	15 %
Saturated Fat 1 g	7 %
Trans Fat 0 g	
Monounsaturated Fat 0 g	
Cholesterol 65 mg	22 %
Sodium 467 mg	19 %
Total Carbohydrates 82 g	27 %
Dietary Fiber 11 g	44 %
Sugars 14 g	
Protein 41 g	
Vitamin A 70 %	Vitamin C 119 %
Calcium 15 %	Iron 30 %
Vitamin K 28 mcg	
Potassium 1229 mg	
Magnesium 204 mg	

Salads

Cole Slaw

Servings = 6
Serving size = about 1 Cup

This recipe can easily be multiplied, but you'll have a lot of Cole Slaw. This recipe keeps well in the refrigerator for about 24 hours.

1/4 tsp.	celery seed
1 Tbsp.	all purpose flour
1/2 tsp.	dry mustard
1 1/2 tsp.	granulated sugar
1	egg yolk
1/8 tsp.	cayenne pepper
1/2 Cup	2% milk
1/4 tsp.	salt
2 Tbsp.	white wine vinegar
1 small	head white cabbage

Place celery seed, flour, dry mustard, granulated sugar, egg yolk, cayenne pepper, salt and milk in a blender.

Blend on low while slowly adding the vinegar.

Transfer contents of blender to a sauce pan and heat over high heat whisking continuously. As the sauce heats check the temperature with a thermometer. When it reaches 140°F it will begin to thicken. Remove from the heat at 150° and continue whisk for about a minute while it cools.

Chill sauce in the refrigerator for at least 3 hours.

Add chilled sauce to the sliced cabbage. Stir until the cabbage is well coated.

Chill for another hour, then serve.

"Cabbage: A vegetable about as large and wise as a man's head."

Ambrose Bierce, Author

The refrigerator light goes on...
This recipe was made by returning to original cole slaw recipes, which were custard based and not made with a jar of mayonnaise. There are lot of recipes in older cookbooks that can be good for you.

Nutrition Facts	
Serving size	about 1 cup
Servings	6
Calories 51	Calories from Fat 6
	% Daily Value
Total Fat 1 g	1 %
Saturated Fat 0 g	1 %
Trans Fat 0 g	
Monounsaturated Fat 0 g	
Cholesterol 37 mg	13 %
Sodium 131 mg	5 %
Total Carbohydrates 10 g	3 %
Dietary Fiber 3 g	11 %
Sugars 6 g	
Protein 3 g	
Vitamin A 4 %	Vitamin C 64 %
Calcium 9 %	Iron 5 %
Vitamin K 72 mcg	
Potassium 335 mg	
Magnesium 23 mg	

Jicama Salad

Servings = 8
Serving size = about 1 cup

This recipe can easily be multiplied and keeps well in the refrigerator for 2 - 3 days.

1 small	jicama root
2	limes (juiced)
1/2 tsp.	salt
2 tsp.	maple syrup
1/4 Cup	cilantro leaves
1/2 tsp.	ground cumin
4 tsp.	grapeseed oil

After peeling and cutting the jicama into matchstick, place it in a large glass or stainless steel bowl with the lime juice, salt, maple syrup, cilantro, cumin and grapeseed oil.

Toss well and chill for at least 2 hours before serving.

"The best way to lose weight is to close your mouth - something very difficult for a politician. Or watch your food - just watch it, don't eat it."
Edward Koch, Former
Mayor of New York City

The refrigerator light goes on...
Never be afraid to use a new ingredient. The crunch of jicama makes great salads. Its sweet flavor goes great in salads when used raw but also works well in soups and stews much like a turnip or parsnip.

Nutrition Facts	
Serving size	about 1 cup
Servings	8
Calories 59	Calories from Fat 21
	% Daily Value
Total Fat 2 g	4 %
Saturated Fat 0 g	1 %
Trans Fat 0 g	
Monounsaturated Fat 1 g	
Cholesterol 0 mg	0 %
Sodium 149 mg	6 %
Total Carbohydrates 9 g	3 %
Dietary Fiber 4 g	16 %
Sugars 3 g	
Protein 1 g	
Vitamin A 1 %	Vitamin C 33 %
Calcium 1 %	Iron 3 %
Vitamin K 2 mcg	
Potassium 143 mg	
Magnesium 12 mg	

Lemon Vinaigrette

Servings = 4
Serving size = 1 1/2 Tablespoons dressing

This recipe can easily be multiplied and keeps well for up to 4 days in the refrigerator.

2 Tbsp.	extra virgin olive oil
1 Tbsp.	lemon juice
1 tsp.	pure maple syrup
2 tsp.	coarse ground mustard
1/8 tsp.	dried tarragon
1/8 tsp.	salt
to taste	fresh ground black pepper

Place olive oil, lemon juice, maple syrup, mustard, tarragon, salt and pepper in a small bowl and whisk until well blended.

Chill for at least 20 minutes before serving.

"To make a good salad is to be a brilliant diplomatist -- the problem is entirely the same in both cases. To know exactly how much oil one must put with one's vinegar."
Oscar Wilde, Poet

The refrigerator light goes on...
The ingredients for a vinaigrette are more important than with other dressings. Use the highest quality olive oil. I have quality inexpensive oil that I cook with, but a rich, mellow Tuscan oil should be used for a recipe such as this one. There is a difference in price, but it will show in the final flavor of your dressing.

Nutrition Facts	
Serving size	1 1/2 Tablespoons
Servings	4
Calories 68	Calories from Fat 62
	% Daily Value
Total Fat 7 g	11 %
Saturated Fat 1 g	4 %
Trans Fat 0 g	
Monounsaturated Fat 0 g	
Cholesterol 0 mg	0 %
Sodium 101 mg	4 %
Total Carbohydrates 2 g	<1 %
Dietary Fiber <1 g	1 %
Sugars 1 g	
Protein 0 g	
Vitamin A 0 %	Vitamin C 6 %
Calcium 0 %	Iron 1 %
Vitamin K 4 mcg	
Potassium 16 mg	
Magnesium 1 mg	

Red Beans and Rice Chopped Salad

2 **30 min.**

Servings = 2
Serving size = about 3 Cups

This recipe can easily be multiplied but does not make very good leftovers. Cooking time does not include chilling time.

1 Cup	water
1/4 Cup	brown rice
1 tsp.	olive oil
1 large	red onion (diced)
1/2 tsp.	paprika
1/8 tsp.	salt
2 tsp.	no salt added Cajun or Creole seasoning
4 Tbsp.	non-fat Greek yogurt
to taste	fresh ground black pepper
2 Tbsp.	reduced-fat sour cream
2 Tbsp.	2% milk
1/2 tsp.	honey
2	ribs celery (diced)
1 medium	green bell pepper (diced)
3 ounces	Andouille sausage links (sliced into thin half-rounds)
1 15-ounce can	no salt added kidney beans (drained and rinsed)
8	leaves Romaine lettuce (thinly sliced crosswise)

Place the water in a saucepan over high heat. When boiling, add the brown rice, reduce to a simmer and partially cover. Cook for about 25 minutes until tender.

While the rice is cooking, place the olive oil in a medium sauté pan over medium high heat. When hot add the onion. Cook for about 15 minutes, stirring frequently. Adjust the heat so the onion caramelizes and doesn't burn.

When the onions and rice are done, place them together in a small bowl and place the bowl in the refrigerator (or freezer if in a hurry). Stir them occasionally while cooling.

While the onions and rice are cooking, place the paprika, salt, Creole seasoning, yogurt, pepper, sour cream, milk and honey in a small bowl. Stir until blended. Place in the refrigerator to chill.

When the rice, onions and dressing are chilled, place them in a large bowl with the celery, pepper, sausage, beans and lettuce. Toss well and serve.

"A jazz musician can improvise based on his knowledge of music. He understands how things go together. For a chef, once you have that basis, that's when cuisine is truly exciting."
Charlie Trotter, Chef

The refrigerator light goes on...
I am pretty careful about the sausage that I select. Look at the nutrition facts box and choose sausages that come in between 80 and 100 calories in a 2 ounce serving. Then look at the amount of sodium and choose those with sodium levels less than 400mg per 2-ounce serving.

This recipe used a pre-cooked Andouille sausage. The all-natural nitrate free version from Wellshire might not be available to you, however. Look for similar sausage or even a chorizo or other spicy choice.

Nutrition Facts	
Serving size	about 3 cups
Servings	2
Calories 521	Calories from Fat 162
	% Daily Value
Total Fat 17 g	28 %
Saturated Fat 5 g	23 %
Trans Fat 0 g	
Monounsaturated Fat 8 g	
Cholesterol 38 mg	14 %
Sodium 494 mg	19 %
Total Carbohydrates 70 g	22 %
Dietary Fiber 17 g	60 %
Sugars 10 g	
Protein 23 g	
Vitamin A 164 %	Vitamin C 172 %
Calcium 20 %	Iron 42 %
Vitamin K 148 mcg	
Potassium 1459 mg	
Magnesium 146 mg	

Red Potato Salad

Servings = 8
Serving Size = 1/2 Cup salad

This recipe can easily be multiplied. Keeps well for up to 72 hours.

3 quarts	water
2 lbs.	small red potatoes
1/4 Cup	reduced-fat mayonnaise
1/4 Cup	non-fat sour cream
1 Tbsp.	coarse ground mustard
2 Tbsp.	curley parsley
1/4 tsp.	salt
1/8 tsp.	fresh ground black pepper

Place the water in a large stock pot fitted with a steamer basket. Bring the water to a boil over medium-high heat. Steam the potatoes for about 30 minutes until slightly soft. Remove and let cool for about ten minutes and then chill thoroughly in the refrigerator.

Cut the potatoes into 1/2 to 1 inch pieces. Place in mixing bowl and add mayonnaise, sour cream, mustard, parsley, salt and pepper.

Fold together gently and chill well before serving.

"What I say is that, if a man really likes potatoes, he must be a pretty decent sort of fellow."
Winnie the Pooh, Famous Bear

The refrigerator light goes on...
The waxy red potatoes hold together better in a salad than russets. Use Yukon Gold potatoes if you don't want the red skin. The larger red potatoes are easily peeled after boiling – the skins will generally just slip off.

Nutrition Facts	
Serving size	1/2 Cup salad
Servings	8
Calories 120	Calories from Fat 9
	% Daily Value
Total Fat 4 g	6 %
Saturated Fat 1 g	5 %
Trans Fat 0 g	
Monounsaturated Fat 0 g	
Cholesterol 6 mg	2 %
Sodium 154 mg	7 %
Total Carbohydrates 19 g	6 %
Dietary Fiber 2 g	8 %
Sugars 2 g	
Protein 3 g	
Vitamin A 4 %	Vitamin C 40 %
Calcium 3 %	Iron 5 %
Vitamin K 30 mcg	
Potassium 547 mg	
Magnesium 26 mg	

Roasted Tomato Dressing

Servings = 4
Serving size = 3 Tablespoons (makes about 3/4 Cup)

This recipe can easily be multiplied and keeps well in the refrigerator for about 3 days.

6 ounces	cherry or grape tomatoes
1 Tbsp.	extra virgin olive oil
2 Tbsp.	balsamic vinegar
1/4 tsp.	salt
1/8 tsp.	pepper
2 Tbsp.	flat leaf parsley

Place the tomatoes in a medium pan and place the pan in the preheated oven. Roast for about 15 - 20 minutes. Shake the pan about three or four times. The outside of the tomatoes should be slightly browned in spots. Do not roast so long that the tomatoes burst open. If one or two do, it's time to take the pan from the oven.

Place the roasted tomatoes, olive oil, vinegar, salt, pepper and parsley in a mini-chopper or blender (a stick blender will work too).

Process until smooth and then chill for at least an hour.

This goes especially good over spicier greens like arugula (rocket) or watercress.

"Home grown tomatoes, home grown tomatoes
What would life be like without home grown
tomatoes
Only two things that money can't buy
That's true love and home grown tomatoes."
Guy Clark, Songwriter

The refrigerator light goes on...
This dressing is simple, fast and easy. Roasting the tomatoes gives them a lovely umami flavor that's also nice and sweet. Using the smaller tomatoes will give you a good tomato flavor year 'round that you can't get from the awful things that grocery stores sell as tomatoes in the winter months.

Nutrition Facts	
Serving size	3 Tablespoons
Servings	4
Calories 43	Calories from Fat 31
	% Daily Value
Total Fat 3 g	5 %
Saturated Fat 1 g	2 %
Trans Fat 0 g	
Monounsaturated Fat 3 g	
Cholesterol 0 mg	0 %
Sodium 149 mg	6 %
Total Carbohydrates 3 g	1 %
Dietary Fiber 1 g	2 %
Sugars 2 g	
Protein 0 g	
Vitamin A 10 %	Vitamin C 13 %
Calcium 1 %	Iron 2 %
Vitamin K 36 mcg	
Potassium 113 mg	
Magnesium 6 mg	

Salads

Shrimp Salad

4 **30 min.**

Serving size = about 1 Cup salad

This recipe can easily be multiplied by 2. This recipe keeps well for up to 36 hours in the refrigerator and is actually better when made the night before. Serve with a whole wheat dinner roll and a side salad.

	spray olive or grapeseed oil
1 lb.	large shrimp (peeled and deveined)
2	ribs celery (diced)
1 Tbsp.	white onion (minced)
2 Tbsp.	reduced fat mayonnaise
4 Tbsp.	fat free sour cream
1/4 tsp.	salt
2 cloves	garlic (minced)
1 Tbsp.	sweet pickle relish
to taste	fresh ground black pepper
1/8 tsp.	paprika
4 large	tomatoes (cored and seeded)

Place a large skillet over medium-high heat. When the pan is hot spray lightly with the oil and add the shrimp in batches small enough that the individual shrimp don't touch. Cook for about 3 - 4 minutes on each side and remove to a cutting board.

When the shrimp have cooled chop them into large 1/2 inch dice.

Combine the chopped shrimp with the celery, onion, mayonnaise, sour cream, salt, garlic, relish, paprika and black pepper.

Chill well. When ready to serve stuff the tomatoes with equal amounts of shrimp salad.

"The onion is the truffle of the poor."
Robert J. Courtine, Editor:
Larousse Gastronomique

The refrigerator light goes on...
Shrimp salad was the summer special meal when I was a teenager. I lived near the shore and there's nothing better than the simple combination of shrimp with celery, pickle relish and a little paprika stuffed into a hollowed out tomato to make it feel like summer. Unless, of course, it's the corn on the cob.... This variation is quick and easy and low in fat.

Nutrition Facts	
Serving size	about 1 Cup salad
Servings	4
Calories 210	Calories from Fat 53
	% Daily Value
Total Fat 6 g	9 %
Saturated Fat 1 g	7 %
Trans Fat 0 g	
Monounsaturated Fat 1 g	
Cholesterol 180 mg	60 %
Sodium 437 mg	18 %
Total Carbohydrates 14 g	5 %
Dietary Fiber 3 g	13 %
Sugars 8 g	
Protein 22 g	
Vitamin A 47 %	Vitamin C 54 %
Calcium 11 %	Iron 19 %
Vitamin K 39 mcg	
Potassium 835 mg	
Magnesium 70 mg	

Spinach Salad with Ginger Dressing and Sesame Chicken

3 **45 min.**

Serving size = 4 ounces chicken with salad

This recipe can easily be multiplied by 2 or 3. Makes great sandwiches the next day.

2 Tbsp.	grapeseed oil
1/4 Cup	frozen orange juice concentrate (thawed)
1/8 tsp.	salt
1/8 tsp.	fresh ground black pepper
2 Tbsp.	crystallized ginger (minced)
1 tsp.	minced parsley
1 Tbsp.	minced chives
3 Tbsp.	slivered almonds
3 Tbsp.	black sesame seeds
3	4-ounce boneless skinless chicken breasts (cut into 1 inch strips)
	spray olive oil
1/8 tsp.	salt
9 ounces	baby spinach
1 15-ounce can	mandarin oranges (drained of all syrup)
1/2 small	red onion (sliced as thinly as possible)

Place the grapeseed oil, orange juice concentrate, salt, pepper, ginger, parsley and chives in a mini chopper or blender. Process until smooth and chill.

Preheat the oven to 425°F. Place a medium sized skillet in the oven.

Place the almonds in a small skillet over medium heat. Cook, tossing frequently, until slightly browned and remove from the heat.

Place the sesame seeds on a sheet of waxed paper. Place the chicken strips one at a time in the sesame seeds to coat just one side of each strip.

Remove the hot pan from the oven and spray lightly with olive oil. Place the chicken strips in the pan with the coated side down. Sprinkle the 1/8 teaspoon salt over the uncoated side and return the pan to the oven. After about 7 minutes turn the chicken strips over. The chicken will take another 8 - 10 minutes to cook.

While the chicken is cooking place the spinach in a large bowl with the chilled dressing. Toss until well coated. Divide between three plates. Sprinkle the mandarin oranges around the plate and then top with the toasted almonds and sliced red onion.

When the chicken is done place the strips on top of the salad and serve.

"On the subject of spinach: divide into little piles. Rearrange again into new piles. After five or six maneuvers, sit back and say you are full."
Delia Ephron, Writer

The refrigerator light goes on...
This is a lovely spring salad with everything. Healthy fats, lean meats, nuts, seeds, fruit, fiber, vitamins.... It's an easy weeknight meal but the chicken can be made ahead and the salad served for a dinner party with quick assembly.

Nutrition Facts		
Serving size	4 oz. chicken with salad	
Servings		3
Calories 393	Calories from Fat 167	
		% Daily Value
Total Fat 19 g		30 %
Saturated Fat 2 g		11 %
Trans Fat 0 g		
Monounsaturated Fat 6 g		
Cholesterol 66 mg		22 %
Sodium 346 mg		14 %
Total Carbohydrates 24 g		8 %
Dietary Fiber 5 g		22 %
Sugars 15 g		
Protein 33 g		
Vitamin A 181 %	Vitamin C 36 %	
Calcium 15 %	Iron 25 %	
Vitamin K 422 mcg		
Potassium 1148 mg		
Magnesium 161 mg		

Salads

Thai Cucumber Salad

Servings = 4
Serving Size = 1 Cup

This recipe can easily be multiplied, but leftovers are good for no more than 24 hours.

1 Cup	rice vinegar
1 tsp.	lime zest (minced)
1/4 tsp.	Tabasco sauce
2 Tbsp.	Splenda or stevia
1/2 Cup	red onion (diced)
2 large	cucumbers (sliced)
1/4 Cup	cilantro leaves
1 Tbsp.	raw peanuts

Combine the rice vinegar, lime zest, Tabasco, Splenda or stevia, red onion, cucumber slices and cilantro leaves in a glass or stainless steel bowl.

You can add the peanuts now and let them marinate. They will be slightly chewy when the salad is served. I prefer to sprinkle them over the top of the salad when I am serving.

Marinate at least 2 hours.

"A spoonful of honey will catch more flies than a gallon of vinegar."

Benjamin Franklin, American Statesman

The refrigerator light goes on...
When I was a kid in Atlanta my mom used to make cucumbers and onions with white vinegar, a touch of salt and pepper and just enough sugar to take the bite off. The flavors are the same – Southeast America, Southeast Asia – just subtle differences.

Nutrition Facts	
Serving size	1 Cup
Servings	4
Calories 46	Calories from Fat 11
	% Daily Value
Total Fat 1 g	2 %
Saturated Fat 1 g	1 %
Trans Fat 0 g	
Monounsaturated Fat 0 g	
Cholesterol 0 mg	0 %
Sodium 8 mg	0 %
Total Carbohydrates 5 g	2 %
Dietary Fiber 1 g	5 %
Sugars 3 g	
Protein 1 g	
Vitamin A 3 %	Vitamin C 10 %
Calcium 3 %	Iron 3 %
Vitamin K 10 mcg	
Potassium 229 mg	
Magnesium 21 mg	

Vegetarian Corn and Black Bean Taco Salad

2 **45 min.**

Serving size = 1 large salad

This recipe can easily be multiplied by 2 or 3. The corn and black bean mixture will keep well in the refrigerator for about 2 days.

1 tsp.	olive oil
1 medium	onion (diced)
1 medium	green bell pepper (diced)
1/2 tsp.	chili powder
1/2 tsp.	cumin
1/8 tsp.	salt
1	ear corn (kernels cut from cob)
1 15-ounce can	no salt added black beans (drained and rinsed)
1/4 Cup	water
2 ounces	unsalted corn tortilla chips
3 Cups	iceberg lettuce (sliced thin)
1 large	tomato (sliced into small wedges)
2 ounces	reduced fat Monterey Jack cheese (shredded)
2 Tbsp.	reduced fat sour cream

Place a large skillet over medium heat and add the oil. Add the diced onion. Cook, stirring frequently, until the onions begin to soften. Add the green bell pepper, chili powder, cumin and salt. Cook for about 3 minutes until the peppers begin to soften.

Add the corn and cook for about 3 minutes. Add the black beans and the water and continue cooking for about 7 - 10 minutes over medium heat until the water is almost evaporated. Remove from the heat, let cool and then refrigerate.

While the corn and black bean mixture is cooling slice the lettuce and the tomatoes. Shred the cheese.

When ready to assemble place the broken taco shells in the bottom of a large bowl. Top with the lettuce and then the corn and black bean mixture. Arrange the tomato wedges around the edges.

Top with the shredded cheese, then spoon the sour cream on top and serve.

"Texas: 32 electoral votes, another of the so-called big enchiladas or if not an enchilada at least a huge taco."

Dan Rather, Newsman

The refrigerator light goes on...
I've had requests for a vegetarian version of my Taco Salad recipe and here it is. I have tried this with frozen corn (about a cup), and that'll work in a pinch, but it's just not as good as using fresh corn. There are endless variations for this recipe. You could use pinto beans and rice. Substitute with anaheim or poblano peppers for a spicier mix. Red peppers will make it sweeter.

I like to use broken corn taco shells in this salad - they hold up better when the dish gets to the table. Lastly, you can add your favorite bottled salsa. Choose one that has very low sodium and little added sugar.

Nutrition Facts	
Serving size	1 large salad
Servings	2
Calories 550	Calories from Fat 120
	% Daily Value
Total Fat 14 g	21 %
Saturated Fat 6 g	30 %
Trans Fat 0 g	
Monounsaturated Fat 4 g	
Cholesterol 26 mg	9 %
Sodium 375 mg	16 %
Total Carbohydrates 86 g	29 %
Dietary Fiber 17 g	68 %
Sugars 12 g	
Protein 28 g	
Vitamin A 36 %	Vitamin C 120 %
Calcium 39 %	Iron 36 %
Vitamin K 43 mcg	
Potassium 1474 mg	
Magnesium 168 mg	

Zucchini Salad

Servings = 4
Serving size = about 1 1/2 Cups

This recipe can easily be multiplied and keeps well for about 48 hours.

2 Tbsp.	olive oil
2 Tbsp.	balsamic vinegar
2 Tbsp.	maple syrup
1/4 tsp.	salt
to taste	fresh ground black pepper
1 tsp.	dried marjoram
1 lb.	zucchini (cut into medium dice)
8 ounces	grape or cherry tomatoes
4 Tbsp.	pine nuts

Whisk together the olive oil, balsamic vinegar, maple syrup, salt, pepper and marjoram. Place in the refrigerator while cutting the zucchini.

Cut the zucchini into medium dice. This should be about 1/4 inch cubes.

Toss the zucchini, tomatoes and pine nuts together in the vinaigrette. Chill well before serving.

"To remember a successful salad is generally to remember a successful dinner; at all events, the perfect dinner necessarily includes the perfect salad."

George Ellwanger,
Gastronomist

The refrigerator light goes on...
I love this little salad. It's quick and easy and really tasty. You can use yellow squash instead or combine the two for great color. It makes a great side dish for almost any soup and then you have the perfect dinner.

Nutrition Facts	
Serving size	about 1 1/2 Cups
Servings	4
Calories 178	Calories from Fat 111
	% Daily Value
Total Fat 13 g	20 %
Saturated Fat 1 g	7 %
Trans Fat 0 g	
Monounsaturated Fat 7 g	
Cholesterol 41 mg	14 %
Sodium 162 mg	7 %
Total Carbohydrates 15 g	5 %
Dietary Fiber 2 g	9 %
Sugars 11 g	
Protein 3 g	
Vitamin A 14 %	Vitamin C 44 %
Calcium 4 %	Iron 7 %
Vitamin K 19 mcg	
Potassium 508 mg	
Magnesium 49 mg	

Beef Tips in Brown Gravy

4 **45 min.**

Serving size = 4 ounces beef with sauce and 2 ounces noodles

This recipe can easily be multiplied and makes great leftovers.

3 tsp.	olive oil
1 lb.	button mushrooms (sliced)
2 lbs.	onions (sliced)
1 lb.	top round or other lean beef (cut into 1/2 inch strips)
1 1/4 Cup	water (divided)
1/2 tsp.	salt
to taste	fresh ground black pepper
1 Tbsp.	Worcestershire sauce
3 quarts	water
8 ounces	whole wheat spaghetti
1 Tbsp.	cornstarch

Place 2 teaspoons olive oil in a large skillet over high heat. Add the mushrooms and cook for about 10 minutes, tossing frequently.

When the mushrooms are browned and well caramelized, remove them to a plate. Add 1 teaspoon olive oil to the pan and then the sliced onions. Cook, stirring frequently, until well browned.

Add the beef and cook until browned.

Add the cooked mushrooms, 1 cup water, salt, pepper and Worcestershire sauce. Stir and cover. Reduce the heat to medium low and simmer for about 30 minutes. Stir occasionally.

After about 20 minutes of cooking, place the water in a medium stock pot over high heat. When the water is boiling, add the pasta. Cook for about 12 minutes until done.

When the pasta is ready to serve, place 1/4 cup cold water in a small dish with the cornstarch. Stir until dissolved. Add the mixture to the pan with the beef. Stir until thickened.

Drain the pasta and serve topped with the beef tips and gravy.

"Ask not what you can do for your country. Ask what's for lunch."
Orson Welles, Actor

The refrigerator light goes on...
This is a recipe that I remember from my childhood. I am not sure how my mother made it but I can remember the taste and this is it. A rich umami flavor from the caramelized mushrooms and onions combine with the beef for that great comfort food flavor. Perfect for a cold winter's night.

Nutrition Facts	
Serving size	4 ounces beef with sauce and 2 ounces noodles
Servings	4
Calories 193	Calories from Fat 83
	% Daily Value
Total Fat 9 g	114 %
Saturated Fat 2 g	12 %
Trans Fat 0 g	
Monounsaturated Fat 5 g	
Cholesterol 62 mg	21 %
Sodium 420 mg	17 %
Total Carbohydrates 67 g	22 %
Dietary Fiber 10 g	38 %
Sugars 12 g	
Protein 40 g	
Vitamin A 0 %	Vitamin C 32 %
Calcium 10 %	Iron 31 %
Vitamin K 4 mcg	
Potassium 1243 mg	
Magnesium 141 mg	

Chicken Leek Risotto

2 **30 min.**

Serving Size = 4 ounces salmon

This recipe can easily be multiplied and makes good leftovers. Reheat gently.

1 tsp.	olive oil
2 large	leeks (cleaned and sliced)
1/2 Cup	arborio rice
1/8 tsp.	dried tarragon
2 Cups	water
1/4 tsp.	saffron threads
to taste	fresh ground black pepper
8 ounces	boneless skinless chicken breast (sliced into strips)
1 ounce	Parmigiano-Reggiano (grated)

Place the olive oil in a medium skillet over medium-high heat. Add the green tops of the leeks and cook stirring frequently. As they get limp add the white part of the leek and cook for another few minutes until they are just limp.

Add the Arborio rice and the tarragon and stir. Cook for about two minutes and add the water stir.

Add the saffron, salt, pepper and stir. Reduce the heat to medium-low and simmer the rice for about 15 minutes. Check the doneness of the rice occasionally. Add more water 1/4 cup at a time as needed.

As the rice is almost done add the chicken and another 1/4 cup water. Stir, increase the heat to medium and cook for about 5 minutes until the chicken is cooked through. Add the grated Parmigiano and stir until blended. Serve.

"If you can mock a leek, you can eat a leek."
William Shakespeare,
Playwright

The refrigerator light goes on...
I do love saffron and it is pretty expensive, especially when you look at the price per pound. The great thing is that it doesn't take much saffron to add a lot of flavor. Twenty threads or so is about 1/4 teaspoon and will add a ton of flavor to your recipes.

Nutrition Facts	
Serving size	about 2 1/2 Cups
Servings	2
Calories 486	Calories from Fat 71
	% Daily Value
Total Fat 8 g	12 %
Saturated Fat 3 g	16 %
Trans Fat 0 g	
Monounsaturated Fat 3 g	
Cholesterol 74 mg	25 %
Sodium 333 mg	14 %
Total Carbohydrates 65 g	22 %
Dietary Fiber 5 g	18 %
Sugars 7 g	
Protein 37 g	
Vitamin A 61 %	Vitamin C 38 %
Calcium 29 %	Iron 38 %
Vitamin K 86 mcg	
Potassium 659 mg	
Magnesium 99 mg	

Chicken with Creamy Red Pepper Flakes Sauce

2 **30 min.**

Serving size = 4 ounces chicken with pasta and sauce

This recipe can easily be multiplied but does not make very good leftovers.

1 quart	water
2 ounces	whole wheat fettuccine
2 tsp.	olive oil (divided)
8 ounces	boneless skinless chicken breast
1 large	shallot (minced)
1/2 large	red bell pepper (diced)
1 large	ear corn (shuck kernels from cob)
2 ounces	pepperoncini (diced)
1/2 tsp.	dried red pepper flakes
1/4 Cup	white wine
1/4 Cup	2% milk
1 ounce	goat cheese
1/4 tsp.	salt
to taste	fresh ground black pepper

Place the water in a large stock pot over high heat.

When the water boils, add the pasta to the water.

Cut the chicken into 1/2 inch strips.

While the pasta is cooking, place one teaspoon olive oil in a large skillet over medium high heat.

Add the chicken to the pan and cook for about 5 to 7 minutes, turning at least once. When the chicken is just cooked through, remove to a plate.

Add the second teaspoon olive oil to the pan and then the shallots and red bell peppers. Cook for about 2 minutes and then add the corn, pepperoncini and red pepper flakes. Cook for about 3 minutes, stirring frequently.

Add the white wine and cook for about 1 minute. Reduce the heat to medium.

Add the chicken, milk, goat cheese, salt and pepper. Stir while the cheese melts.

Drain the pasta and add the fettuccine to the pan. Toss well and serve.

"It's like spicy food - sometimes you have to tone it down so more people can enjoy it."
Kenneth Edmonds, Musician

The refrigerator light goes on...
OK, I'll admit it. I actually made this with a full teaspoon of red pepper flakes. It's pretty spicy with that much, but it is not so overwhelming that you can't taste all of the other ingredients. If you don't like spicy food, you might use 1/4 teaspoon.

Nutrition Facts		
Serving size	4 oz. chicken w/pasta	
Servings		2
Calories 454	Calories from Fat 110	
		% Daily Value
Total Fat 12 g		22 %
Saturated Fat 4 g		17 %
Trans Fat 0 g		
Monounsaturated Fat 4 g		
Cholesterol 79 mg		25 %
Sodium 478 mg		21 %
Total Carbohydrates 46 g		16 %
Dietary Fiber 5 g		17 %
Sugars 5 g		
Protein 37 g		
Vitamin A 34 %	Vitamin C 86 %	
Calcium 10 %	Iron 17 %	
Vitamin K 5 mcg		
Potassium 825 mg		
Magnesium 124 mg		

Cottage Pie

2 **90 min.**

Serving size = 1 pie (about 3 Cups)

This recipe can easily be multiplied and makes good leftovers. Reheat gently.

3 quarts	water
8 ounces	yukon gold potatoes (peeled)
1 tsp.	olive oil
1 small	onion (diced)
12 ounces	95% lean ground beef
2 tsp.	cornstarch
1 large	carrot (peeled and diced)
1	rib celery (diced)
1 Tbsp.	tomato paste
1/8 tsp.	salt
1 Tbsp.	Worcestershire sauce
1 Cup	low sodium beef broth
2 tsp.	unsalted butter
2 Tbsp	non-fat buttermilk
2 Tbsp	2% milk
to taste	fresh ground black pepper

Place the water in a large stock pot over high heat.

Quarter the potatoes and add to the stock pot. Cover with water by about an inch. Bring to boil and then reduce heat until the water is simmering.

Cook the potatoes about 15 – 20 minutes until slightly soft in the middle. They should give when squeezed.

Preheat the oven to 300°F.

While the potatoes are cooking, place the olive oil in a medium sauce pan over medium heat. Add the onions and cook for about 3 minutes until they begin to soften.

Add the ground beef and cook, stirring frequently, until browned.

Sprinkle the cornstarch over the ground beef and stir in. Add the carrot, celery, tomato paste, salt, Worces-tershire sauce and beef stock. Stir, cover and place the pot in the oven.

When the potatoes are done, remove from heat and drain the water. Pass the potatoes through a ricer or mash gently with a fork until smooth.

Add butter, buttermilk, milk and salt and stir in. Add ground black pepper to taste.

After an hour of cooking in the oven, remove the beef and divide between two bowls (you can make this in one Pyrex dish also). Top with the potatoes and return to the oven. Bake for about 10 minutes and serve.

"Food is the most primitive form of comfort."
Sheilah Graham, Gossip Columnist

The refrigerator light goes on...
Cottage Pie is essentially the same as Shepherd's Pie. Cottage Pie is made with beef and Shepherd's Pie with lamb (makes sense). This is English comfort food at its best: a delicious warm stew topped with mashed potatoes. What could be better?

Nutrition Facts		
Serving size	1 pie (about 3 Cups)	
Servings		2
Calories 272	Calories from Fat 117	
		% Daily Value
Total Fat 13 g		20 %
Saturated Fat 6 g		29 %
Trans Fat 0 g		
Monounsaturated Fat 6 g		
Cholesterol 81 mg		27 %
Sodium 418 mg		17 %
Total Carbohydrates 46 g		15 %
Dietary Fiber 5 g		18 %
Sugars 7 g		
Protein 31 g		
Vitamin A 109 %	Vitamin C 30 %	
Calcium 10 %	Iron 24 %	
Vitamin K 17 mcg		
Potassium 1393 mg		
Magnesium 74 mg		

Crab Cakes

 4 **30 min.**

Serving size = 2 crab cakes

This recipe is easily multiplied. Uncooked crab cakes do not keep very well past about 24 hours. Cooked crab cakes will make good sandwiches the next day.

Serve with Plain Mashed Potatoes and Pan Grilled Broccoli (recipes included).

1 lb.	lump crabmeat
1/3 Cup	low-sodium saltine crackers
1/2 tsp.	Tabasco sauce
2 tsp.	Worcestershire sauce
1 Tbsp.	shallot (minced)
2 tsp.	Dijon mustard
1 large	egg white
1	rib celery (diced)
1 Tbsp.	fresh lemon juice
2 Tbsp.	reduced-fat mayonnaise
1/8 tsp.	salt
to taste	fresh ground black pepper
2 tsp.	extra virgin olive oil

Pick over crabmeat, removing any shell.

Break the saltines into about 1/4 inch pieces.

Fold the crabmeat together with the crumbled saltines. Add Tabasco sauce, Worcestershire sauce, shallot, mustard, egg white, celery, lemon juice, mayonnaise, salt and pepper.

Fold together gently until well blended. Be careful to not break up the crabmeat too much.

Form into 8 cakes and chill. The cakes can be made up to 12 hours in advance.

Preheat the oven to 400° F.

Place the oil in a large non-stick skillet over high heat until the oil is almost smoking.

Place cakes in the hot oil and cook over medium-high heat for about three minutes until brown. Turn and cook for about 2 minutes. Place in hot oven. Cook for another 9 – 10 minutes. Serve.

"Give a man a fish and he has food for a day; teach him how to fish and you can get rid of him for the entire weekend."

Zenna Schaffer, Author

The refrigerator light goes on...
Searing foods requires a good non-stick pan at a very high heat and a small amount of oil.

Nutrition Facts	
Serving size	2 crab cakes
Servings	4
Calories 168	Calories from Fat 55
	% Daily Value
Total Fat 6 g	9 %
Saturated Fat 1 g	5 %
Trans Fat 0 g	
Monounsaturated Fat 2 g	
Cholesterol 90 mg	30 %
Sodium 491 mg	20 %
Total Carbohydrates 5 g	2 %
Dietary Fiber 0 g	1 %
Sugars 1 g	
Protein 22 g	
Vitamin A 1 %	Vitamin C 9 %
Calcium 11 %	Iron 8 %
Vitamin K 13 mcg	
Potassium 430 mg	
Magnesium 42 mg	

Cumin Dusted Flank Steak with Black Beans

2 **30 min.**

Serving size = 4 ounces flank steak with black beans

This recipe can easily be multiplied and makes good leftovers, especially as salad. Thinly slice the beef and toss into the beans.

1 tsp	olive oil
1 medium	onion (diced)
1 15-ounce can	no salt added black beans (drained and rinsed)
1/2 medium	yellow pepper (diced)
1/2	lime (juiced)
1/2 tsp	chili powder
1 1/2 tsp	ground cumin
1/8 tsp	cayenne pepper
1/4 tsp	salt
to taste	fresh ground black pepper
3 medium	green onions (sliced crosswise)
2 4 ounce	flank steak filets spray oil

"To eat steak rare... represents both a nature and a morality."

Roland Barthes, Philosopher

The refrigerator light goes on...
Simple, simple, simple. This great steak dish takes all of about 20 or 25 minutes to make and is so satisfying. If you want it a bit spicier, you can add more (or less) cayenne pepper, but your favorite hot sauce can give it an altogether different flavor.

Place a large skillet in the oven and preheat to 425°F.

While the oven is preheating place the olive oil in a second large skillet over medium-high heat. Add the onion and cook for about 5 minutes stirring frequently.

Add the black beans and cook for about 3 minutes.

Add the yellow pepper, lime juice, chili powder, 1/2 teaspoon ground cumin, cayenne pepper, salt and pepper and toss well. Reduce the heat to low. Add the green onions and toss.

Dust the steaks with the remaining 1 teaspoon ground cumin. Remove the pan from the oven and spray with oil. Place the steaks in the pan and return the pan to the oven. Cook on the first side for about 8 – 9 minutes.

Turn and cook for another 6 – 8 minutes. Remove the steak from the oven and let rest for about 3 minutes. Slice and serve the steak with the black beans.

Nutrition Facts	
Serving size 4 oz. flank steak w/beans	
Servings	2
Calories 411	Calories from Fat 94
	% Daily Value
Total Fat 11 g	16 %
Saturated Fat 3 g	17 %
Trans Fat 0 g	
Monounsaturated Fat 5 g	
Cholesterol 48 mg	16 %
Sodium 374 mg	16 %
Total Carbohydrates 43 g	14 %
Dietary Fiber 9 g	37 %
Sugars 1 g	
Protein 38 g	
Vitamin A 13 %	Vitamin C 272 %
Calcium 15 %	Iron 42 %
Vitamin K 55 mcg	
Potassium 1285 mg	
Magnesium 117 mg	

Eggplant Risotto

2 **30 min.**

Serving size = about 2 Cups

This recipe is easily multiplied and makes great leftovers.

2 tsp.	olive oil
1 clove	garlic (sliced)
1 small	onion (sliced)
1 large	eggplant (cut into 1 inch cubes)
1/4 tsp.	dried tarragon
1/2 tsp.	dried oregano
1/2 tsp.	dried basil
1/2 tsp.	dried rosemary
1/2 Cup	arborio rice
to taste	fresh ground black pepper
3 Cups	water
4 ounces	cherry or grape tomatoes
1 ounce	Parmigiano-Reggiano (grated)
2 ounces	fresh mozzarella (cut into small dice)

Place the olive oil in a medium sized skillet over medium-high heat. Add the garlic and onion and cook for about one minute. Stir frequently.

Add the eggplant and cook, stirring frequently. Adjust the heat as needed to keep the eggplant from burning but turn a nut brown.

Add the dried tarragon, oregano, basil, rosemary and arborio rice and cook for about one minute.

Add the pepper, water, and tomatoes. Stir once and reduce the heat until the rice is simmering. Cook for about 15 minutes until the rice is tender.

Add the parmesan and stir until blended. Serve the risotto topped with the fresh mozzarella cubes.

"Washington, DC is to lying what Wisconsin is to cheese."

Dennis Miller, Comedian

The refrigerator light goes on...
I was having a discussion recently about how to create great low-sodium recipes and this is a great example. There's no added salt but there are a lot of salty flavors. The parmesan and mozzarella add a lot of this. The other key is that there are so many umami flavors – onions, eggplant and the cheeses. The blend of these flavors are enhanced by the herbs. The result is that there's less need for added salt. Best of all, the rich creaminess of the risotto makes for a lovely sauce.

Nutrition Facts	
Serving size	about 2 Cups
Servings	2
Calories 485	Calories from Fat 148
	% Daily Value
Total Fat 17 g	26 %
Saturated Fat 7 g	36 %
Trans Fat 0 g	
Monounsaturated Fat 7 g	
Cholesterol 32 mg	11 %
Sodium 482 mg	20 %
Total Carbohydrates 64 g	21 %
Dietary Fiber 11 g	44 %
Sugars 10 g	
Protein 23 g	
Vitamin A 18 %	Vitamin C 28 %
Calcium 37 %	Iron 23 %
Vitamin K 25 mcg	
Potassium 1021 mg	
Magnesium 71 mg	

Fish Sandwiches with Sun Dried Tomato Tartar Sauce

4 **30 min.**

Serving size = 1 sandwich

"When you fish for love, bait with your heart, not your brain."

Mark Twain

This recipe can easily be multiplied or divided by 2 or 4. The extra tartar sauce keeps well for 3-4 days in the refrigerator. Cooked leftover fish should be allowed to cool and then kept in the refrigerator at most 2 days. Makes great cold sandwiches or can be added to salads.

The refrigerator light goes on...
Tartar Sauce is, of course, the standard with your fish, but that doesn't mean that you can't spice it up every now and then.

2 Tbsp.	reduced-fat sour cream
1 Tbsp.	reduced-fat mayonnaise
1 Tbsp.	pickle relish
1 Tbsp.	sun dried tomato paste
2 Tbsp.	red bell pepper (finely diced)
2 Tbsp.	fresh chives (minced)
1/8 tsp.	salt
to taste	fresh ground black pepper
2 tsp.	olive oil
4 4 ounce	white fish filets (grouper, cod, or halibut)
4	whole wheat hamburger buns
4	leaves iceberg lettuce
4	slices tomato

Mix the sour cream, mayonnaise, pickle relish, tomato paste, bell pepper, chives, salt, and pepper together and place in the refrigerator to chill.

Place a medium skillet on the range over medium high heat. Add the olive oil.

When the oil is hot add the fish to the pan.

Cook for about 5 to 7 minutes on each side.

Serve the fish on buns with 2 Tablespoons tartar sauce, lettuce, and tomato.

Nutrition Facts	
Serving size	1 sandwich
Servings	4
Calories 279	Calories from Fat 60
	% Daily Value
Total Fat 7 g	11 %
Saturated Fat 1 g	5 %
Trans Fat 0 g	
Monounsaturated Fat 2 g	
Cholesterol 40 mg	14 %
Sodium 462 mg	20 %
Total Carbohydrates 25 g	9 %
Dietary Fiber 3 g	13 %
Sugars 7 g	
Protein 28 g	
Vitamin A 16 %	Vitamin C 15 %
Calcium 10 %	Iron 11 %
Vitamin K 17 mcg	
Potassium 794 mg	
Magnesium 138 mg	

Ginger Chicken Satay with Peanut Sauce

6 **30 min.**

Serving size = 4 ounces chicken with sauce

This recipe can easily be multiplied by 2, 3 or 4. The sauce makes 36 servings and keeps well in the refrigerator for 4-5 days. The cooked chicken keeps well for up to 3 days in the refrigerator. Reheat gently or use in sandwiches.

Serve with Coconut Rice (recipe included).

3 Tbsp.	fresh ginger (peeled and finely minced)
3 tsp.	sesame oil
1 1/2 lbs.	boneless skinless chicken breast (cut into 2-ounce strips)
12	wooden skewers
1/4 Cup	smooth peanut butter
6 Tbsp.	low sodium chicken broth
1/2 tsp.	low sodium soy sauce
1/8 tsp.	salt
1/4 cup.	cilantro leaves
	spray olive oil

Place the chicken strips onto skewers.

Combine the minced ginger, sesame oil and chicken together in a large zipper bag. Marinate for at least 4 hours (overnight is best).

While the chicken is marinating place the peanut butter, chicken stock, salt and cilantro in a blender. Puree until smooth. Chill.

When ready to cook, place a large grill pan or skillet over high heat. When the pan is hot, reduce the heat to medium high and spray with oil.

Place the marinated chicken on the grill pan and cook for about 5 minutes. Turn and cook for another 7 to 12 minutes. Serve with peanut sauce.

"Not only is New York City the nation's melting pot, it is also the casserole, the chafing dish and the charcoal grill."

John Lindsay, Mayor

The refrigerator light goes on...
I love this spin on chicken satay with the ginger. It gives it a fresh, light flavor. The peanut sauce with the addition of cilantro is rich but soft and light enough for those with acid reflux.

Nutrition Facts	
Serving size	4 ounces chicken with sauce
Servings	6
Calories 138	Calories from Fat 24
	% Daily Value
Total Fat 3 g	4 %
Saturated Fat 1 g	3 %
Trans Fat 0 g	
Monounsaturated Fat 1 g	
Cholesterol 65 mg	22 %
Sodium 84 mg	4 %
Total Carbohydrates 0 g	0 %
Dietary Fiber 0 g	0 %
Sugars 0 g	
Protein 26 g	
Vitamin A 1 %	Vitamin C 2 %
Calcium 1 %	Iron 5 %
Vitamin K 1 mcg	
Potassium 302 mg	
Magnesium 34 mg	

Grilled Beefsteak with Mushroom Vinaigrette

2 **30 min.**

Serving size = 4 ounces steak with mushrooms

This recipe can easily be multiplied and makes great leftovers as sandwiches.

Serve with a Baked Sweet Potato (recipe included).

2 ounces	crimini or other wild mushrooms
4 tsp.	extra virgin olive oil
1 tsp.	white wine vinegar
1 tsp.	maple syrup
1/8 tsp.	dried tarragon
1/4 tsp.	salt
to taste	fresh ground black pepper
8 ounces	skirt steak or flank steak

Thinly slice the mushrooms into matchsticks.

Place the mushrooms in a bowl and add the olive oil, vinegar, maple syrup, tarragon, 1/8 teaspoon salt and the pepper.

Toss well.

Place a large skillet in the oven and preheat to 375°F.

Sprinkle the remaining 1/8 teaspoon salt over the steak.

When the pan is hot add the steak. Cook for about 7 minutes and turn over. Cook for another 4 to 6 minutes.

Serve the steak topped with the mushroom vinaigrette.

"Bad cooks -- and the utter lack of reason in the kitchen -- have delayed human development longest and impaired it most."

Friedrich Nietzsche,
Philosopher

The refrigerator light goes on...
This is a flavorful but light topping for your grilled steak. Choose more flavorful mushrooms like crimini or shiitaki. It is best to not let the mushrooms marinate too long – about an hour at the most – as they will become mushy. Make the vinaigrette, cook the steak and serve.

Nutrition Facts	
Serving size 4 oz. steak w/mushrooms	
Servings	2
Calories 251 Calories from Fat 137	
	% Daily Value
Total Fat 15 g	22 %
Saturated Fat 3 g	12 %
Trans Fat 0 g	
Monounsaturated Fat 9 g	
Cholesterol 37 mg	12 %
Sodium 354 mg	16 %
Total Carbohydrates 2 g	1 %
Dietary Fiber 0 g	0 %
Sugars 1 g	
Protein 0 g	
Vitamin A 0 %	Vitamin C 0 %
Calcium 4 %	Iron 8 %
Vitamin K 6 mcg	
Potassium 397 mg	
Magnesium 26 mg	

Mussels with Saffron Broth

2 **30 min.**

Serving size = 1 pound mussels with broth and vegetables

This recipe can easily be multiplied but does not make good leftovers.

20	threads saffron
1 Cup	boiling water
3 quarts	water
12 ounces	yams (peeled and cut into 1/2 inch cubes)
2 tsp.	olive oil
1 large	shallot (minced)
1 large	carrot (peeled and diced)
1/2 Cup	white wine
2/3 Cup	frozen peas
to taste	fresh ground black pepper
2 lbs.	mussels (cleaned well)
1 ounce	goat cheese

Place the saffron in a small bowl and add the boiling water.

Place the water in a large stock pot over high heat. When it comes to a boil, add the yams. Cook for about 10 minutes. The yams should be tender but not mushy. Drain the yams and set aside.

Place the olive oil in a large skillet over medium high heat. Add the shallots and cook for one minute. Add the carrot and cook for about two minutes, stirring frequently.

Add the saffron liquid, white wine, peas and pepper. Increase the heat to high.

When the broth is boiling, add the mussels and cover. Cook for about 10 minutes, until the mussels open.

Remove the pan from the heat. Divide the mussels between two large bowls. Place the goat cheese in the pan with the veggies and whisk until melted. Pour the vegetables and broth over the mussels and serve.

"Cogito ergo spud."

The refrigerator light goes on...
I love saffron and thought of this recipe when I was having mussels recently at a restaurant. The broth in the restaurant's dish was good, but it just wasn't tasty enough to eat like a soup. The saffron gives this recipe a rich flowery and savory flavor that's fantastic after eating the mussels. Sort of like having your mussels with built in dessert.

Nutrition Facts	
Serving size	1 lb. mussels with broth and vegetables
Servings	2
Calories 467	Calories from Fat 101
	% Daily Value
Total Fat 11 g	18 %
Saturated Fat 4 g	20 %
Trans Fat 0 g	
Monounsaturated Fat 5 g	
Cholesterol 38 mg	13 %
Sodium 372 mg	16 %
Total Carbohydrates 55 g	22 %
Dietary Fiber 10 g	40 %
Sugars 5 g	
Protein 21 g	
Vitamin A 157 %	Vitamin C 82 %
Calcium 13 %	Iron 35 %
Vitamin K 24 mcg	
Potassium 2006 mg	
Magnesium 98 mg	

Mustard Cornmeal Crusted Fish

4 **30 min.**

Serving size = 4 ounces fish

This recipe can easily be multiplied and makes good leftovers for sandwiches and salads.

Serve with Mashed Yams and Maple Sage Carrots (recipes included).

2 Tbsp.	coarse ground mustard
3 Tbsp.	water
1/8 tsp.	dried tarragon
1/4 tsp.	salt
to taste	fresh ground black pepper
4 Tbsp.	coarse ground yellow cornmeal
4 4-ounce	red snapper filets (or other whitefish)
2 Tbsp.	olive oil

Mix together the mustard, water, tarragon, salt and pepper in small bowl.

Place the cornmeal on a plate.

Dredge the flesh side of each piece of fish in the mustard mixture and then in the cornmeal. Do not coat the skin side of the fish. Place the fish on a plate skin side down.

Pat any remaining cornmeal onto the fish.

Place the oil in a large skillet over medium high heat. When the oil is hot place the fish in the pan, cornmeal side down.

Let the fish cook for about 8 minutes, until the cornmeal coating is crispy, and then turn the fish over. Cook for another 4 to 6 minutes and serve.

"Fishing is boring, unless you catch an actual fish, and then it is disgusting."

Dave Barry

The refrigerator light goes on...
You can use almost any white fish for this: trout, cod, drum, or rockfish. The best part of this recipe is that the crusted fish makes great leftovers as sandwiches and you'll be able to have fish for lunch without any extra work or having to hit the fast food joint.

Nutrition Facts	
Serving size	4 oz. fish
Servings	4
Calories 206	Calories from Fat 80
	% Daily Value
Total Fat 9 g	15 %
Saturated Fat 1 g	4 %
Trans Fat 0 g	
Monounsaturated Fat 5 g	
Cholesterol 42 mg	12 %
Sodium 234 mg	10 %
Total Carbohydrates 6 g	2 %
Dietary Fiber 2 g	4 %
Sugars 0 g	
Protein 24 g	
Vitamin A 4 %	Vitamin C 4 %
Calcium 4 %	Iron 1 %
Vitamin K 4 mcg	
Potassium 506 mg	
Magnesium 50 mg	

Polynesian Chicken

4 **45 min.**

Serving size = 4 ounces chicken breast with sauce

This recipe can easily be multiplied and is great the next day. Reheat gently or use in sandwiches.

Serve with Coconut Rice and Thai Cucumber Salad (recipes included).

3 Tbsp.	low-sodium soy sauce
1 cloves	garlic (minced)
1 tsp.	ground ginger
1 Tbsp.	canola or grapeseed oil
1/2 Cup	pineapple juice
1 Cup	pineapple (diced)
1 Tbsp.	honey
16 ounces	boneless skinless chicken breast (cut into 1/2 inch strips)

Place the soy sauce, minced garlic, ginger, oil, pineapple juice, pineapple chunks and honey in a large glass or stainless bowl and mix well.

Add the chicken strips and mix well. Chill for at least 2 hours (overnight is best).

Preheat oven to 325°F. Place the chicken and sauce in a 12x9 inch oblong pyrex dish. Place the chicken in the oven and cook for about 20 - 25 minutes.

"He is the very pineapple of politeness!"
Richard Brinsley Sheridan,
Playwright

The refrigerator light goes on...
I loved this sort of recipe when I was young. There were a couple of Polynesian restaurants in New Jersey where I went to high school and they had Tiki Huts for tables and served drinks in coconut husks. The sweet, sour, savory flavors always worked so well together. They say that comfort food is what makes you comfortable and I am betting that there are a lot of people who find this one of their comfort food dishes.

Nutrition Facts	
Serving size	4 oz. chicken with sauce
Servings	4
Calories 213	Calories from Fat 44
	% Daily Value
Total Fat 5 g	8 %
Saturated Fat 1 g	3 %
Trans Fat 0 g	
Monounsaturated Fat 3 g	
Cholesterol 65 mg	22 %
Sodium 474 mg	20 %
Total Carbohydrates 15 g	5 %
Dietary Fiber <1 g	1 %
Sugars 11 g	
Protein 27 g	
Vitamin A 1 %	Vitamin C 20 %
Calcium 3 %	Iron 7 %
Vitamin K 3 mcg	
Potassium 407 mg	
Magnesium 45 mg	

Pork Chops with Garlic Sauce

2 **30 min.**

Serving size = 4 ounces pork with sauce

This recipe can easily be multiplied. Leftovers are great for sandwiches. This recipe also requires making Roasted Garlic (recipe included).

Serve with Mashed Yams and Shredded Brussels Sprouts (recipes included).

2 tsp.	olive oil
2 cloves	garlic (thinly sliced)
4 cloves	roasted garlic
1/4 Cup	white wine
3/4 Cup	low sodium chicken broth
1/4 tsp.	salt
to taste	fresh ground black pepper
2 tsp.	unsalted butter
2 4-ounce	pork chops (boneless)
	spray olive oil

Place the olive oil in a small skillet over medium heat. Add the sliced garlic. Cook slowly for about 5 minutes. Reduce the heat to low to keep the garlic from turning brown.

Add the roasted garlic, white wine, chicken stock, salt and pepper. Adjust the heat to medium so that the sauce is at a simmer.

Place a large skillet in the oven and preheat to 425°F.

Simmer for about twenty minutes. Lightly mash the roasted garlic while the sauce is simmering. Cook until the sauce is reduced to about 1/3 cup. Add the butter and reduce the heat to low.

Lightly spray the skillet in the oven with oil. Add the pork chops and return the pan to the oven. Cook on the first side for about 7 – 8 minutes and turn. Cook for another 7 – 8 minutes.

Serve topped with the garlic sauce.

"You can never have enough garlic. With enough garlic, you can eat The New York Times."
Morley Safer, Newsman

The refrigerator light goes on...
This is a lovely sauce and proves that simple ingredients prepared with care can make for the most subtle flavors. Garlic, olive oil, butter... that's all it takes. The slow simmering of the sauce gives it a rich, savory flavor enhanced by the richness of the butter. This goes well with pork but can also top a grilled flank steak or roasted chicken breasts.

Nutrition Facts	
Serving size	4 oz. pork w/sauce
Servings	2
Calories 302	Calories from Fat 150
	% Daily Value
Total Fat 17 g	26 %
Saturated Fat 8 g	29 %
Trans Fat 0 g	
Monounsaturated Fat 4 g	
Cholesterol 72 mg	24 %
Sodium 372 mg	16 %
Total Carbohydrates 5 g	3 %
Dietary Fiber 0 g	1 %
Sugars 0 g	
Protein 27 g	
Vitamin A 3 %	Vitamin C 5 %
Calcium 3 %	Iron 7 %
Vitamin K 4 mcg	
Potassium 613 mg	
Magnesium 31 mg	

Roasted Southwestern Acorn Squash

2 **45 min.**

Serving size = 1 filled squash

This recipe can easily be multiplied but does not make very good leftovers.

1 large	acorn squash (halved and seeded)
1 tsp	olive oil
1 clove	garlic (minced)
1 small	onion (diced)
1	rib celery (diced)
1 small	carrot (peeled and diced)
1 15 ounce can	no salt added black beans (drained and rinsed)
1/2 tsp	ground cumin
1/2 tsp	chili powder
1/8 tsp	salt
to taste	fresh ground black pepper
1 small	red bell pepper (seeded and diced)
1/4 cup	cilantro leaves
3 ounces	Monterey jack cheese (shredded)

"You know, when you get your first asparagus, or your first acorn squash, or your first really good tomato of the season, those are the moments that define the cook's year. I get more excited by that than anything else."

Mario Batali, Chef

The refrigerator light goes on...
Roasted acorn squash is fantastic and so versatile. It makes the perfect side dish but this is a simple and delicious way to get everything good for you in a main course. Beans, veggies, high fiber, great vitamins.... You won't even know that it's good for you.

Preheat the oven to 375°F. Place the acorn squash halves cut side down on a cookie sheet or a large skillet and roast in the oven for about 30 minutes until tender.

While the squash is roasting place the olive oil in a large skillet over medium-high heat. Add the garlic and onions and cook for about 3 - 4 minutes. Add the celery and carrots and cook for another 3 - 4 minutes.

Add the black beans, cumin, chili powder, salt, pepper and diced red pepper. Toss well and cook for about 3 - 4 minutes. Remove from the heat until the squash are finished roasting.

When the squash is roasted spoon the black bean mixture equally into the halves. Top the squash with the shredded cheese and return to the oven for about 5 - 10 minutes until the cheese is melted. Serve.

Nutrition Facts		
Serving size		1 filled squash
Servings		2
Calories 462	Calories from Fat 114	
		% Daily Value
Total Fat 13 g		20 %
Saturated Fat 7 g		33 %
Trans Fat 0 g		
Monounsaturated Fat 4 g		
Cholesterol 27 mg		9 %
Sodium 443 mg		18 %
Total Carbohydrates 65 g		22 %
Dietary Fiber 18 g		71 %
Sugars 6 g		
Protein 27 g		
Vitamin A 149 %	Vitamin C 41 %	
Calcium 44 %	Iron 30 %	
Vitamin K 21 mcg		
Potassium 1579 mg		
Magnesium 190 mg		

Seared Halibut with Basil Oil

2 **30 min.**

Serving size = 4 ounces fish with 1 1/2 tsps. oil

This recipe can easily be multiplied or halved. This recipe does not make very good leftovers.

Serve with Jasmine Rice and Pan Grilled Asparagus (recipes included).

1/4 Cup	extra virgin olive oil
1/2 Cup	fresh basil leaves
2 4 ounce	filets halibut
1/4 tsp.	salt
to taste	fresh ground black pepper
	spray olive oil

Place the olive oil and basil in a blender or mini chopper and process until smooth.

Preheat the oven to 425°F. Place a medium sized skillet in the oven.

While the oven is heating, rinse the halibut filets with cold water and pat dry. Place them on a cutting board skin side up. Cut shallow slits in the skin about 1/4 inch apart. Sprinkle the skin side of the fish with the salt and pepper.

When the oven is hot spray the pan lightly with oil. Place the fish in the pan skin side down. Return the pan to the oven and cook for about 10 - 12 minutes.

Serve the fish skin side up and top with 1 1/2 teaspoons of basil oil.

"You've got bad eating habits if you use a grocery cart in 7-Eleven, okay?"

Dennis Miller, Comedian

The refrigerator light goes on...
This is a simple recipe and you can use the basil oil as an enhancement for almost anything – salmon, cod, chicken breasts, pork tenderloin. This is one of the quickest and easiest yet most elegant meals because of its very simplicity.

Nutrition Facts	
Serving size	4 oz. fish with oil
Servings	2
Calories 183	Calories from Fat 83
	% Daily Value
Total Fat 9 g	14 %
Saturated Fat 1 g	6 %
Trans Fat 0 g	
Monounsaturated Fat 6 g	
Cholesterol 36 mg	12 %
Sodium 351 mg	15 %
Total Carbohydrates 0 g	0 %
Dietary Fiber 0 g	0 %
Sugars 0 g	
Protein 23 g	
Vitamin A 5 %	Vitamin C 0 %
Calcium 6 %	Iron 6 %
Vitamin K 10 mcg	
Potassium 509 mg	
Magnesium 94 mg	

Seared Tuna with Asparagus Salsa

4 **30 min.**

Serving size = 4 ounces tuna with salsa

This recipe can easily be multiplied and makes good leftovers served cold.

Serve with a Baked Sweet Potato (recipe included).

1 lb.	asparagus
	spray olive oil
2 quarts	ice water
1 small	tomato (diced)
1 small	shallot (diced)
1 small	yellow bell pepper (diced)
1 Tbsp.	olive oil
1	lime (juiced)
2 Tbsp.	fresh oregano (coarsely chopped)
1/8 tsp.	cayenne pepper
1/4 tsp.	salt
to taste	fresh ground black pepper
4 4-ounce	tuna steaks
1/2 tsp.	ground cumin

Place a large skillet in the oven and preheat the oven to 375°F.

When the oven is hot, spray the pan with oil and add the asparagus. Cook, turning about twice, for 8 to 10 minutes. Remove and place in the ice water to chill.

When the asparagus is cold, cut it crosswise into small chunks. Leave about 1 inch of the tip of the spears uncut.

Place the asparagus, tomato, shallot, pepper, lime juice, olive oil, oregano, cayenne pepper, salt, pepper in a bowl and mix well. Chill.

Place the skillet back in the oven.

Dust the tuna steaks with ground cumin.

When the pan is again hot, spray it with olive oil. Add the tuna steaks and cook for about 5 to 7 minutes on each side.

Serve topped with salsa.

"Are you casting asparagus on my cooking?"
Curley Howard, Stooge

The refrigerator light goes on...
Salsa is a great way to get veggies without even thinking about it. The pan grilled asparagus makes the perfect salsa and you can serve this with tuna, shrimp... almost any thing you want. It is perfect for tacos. Your family may not even know they are getting a serving of veggies with their meal.

Nutrition Facts	
Serving size	4 oz. tuna with salsa
Servings	4
Calories 208	Calories from Fat 44
	% Daily Value
Total Fat 4 g	5 %
Saturated Fat 1 g	2 %
Trans Fat 0 g	
Monounsaturated Fat 2 g	
Cholesterol 51 mg	16 %
Sodium 193 mg	6 %
Total Carbohydrates 10 g	2 %
Dietary Fiber 2 g	11 %
Sugars 3 g	
Protein 29 g	
Vitamin A 26 %	Vitamin C 149 %
Calcium 6 %	Iron 20 %
Vitamin K 54 mcg	
Potassium 961 mg	
Magnesium 87 mg	

Shrimp Fried Rice

2 **30 min.**

Serving size = about 2 1/2 Cups fried rice

This recipe can easily be multiplied and makes great leftovers.

2 1/2 Cups	water
1/2 Cup	brown rice
2 tsp.	sesame oil
1 medium	white onion (diced)
2 large	carrots (peeled and diced)
1	rib celery (diced)
2/3 Cup	frozen peas (thawed)
6 ounces	shrimp (peeled, deveined and sliced in half lengthwise)
to taste	fresh ground black pepper
3 tsp.	low sodium soy sauce
1 large	egg (beaten)

Place the water in a small sauce pan over high heat. When the water boils, add the rice and reduce the heat to a simmer.

Cook, partially covered, until the water cooks away. Do not stir the rice. When cooked remove from the stove, let cool.

When ready to cook place the sesame oil in a wok or large skillet over high heat. When the oil is nearly smoking, add the onions and carrots. Cook for about 3 to 4 minutes until the onions begin to soften.

Add the peas and shrimp. Cook until the shrimp is pink, stirring frequently. Add the pepper and soy or tamari sauce.

Add the cooked rice and toss until the rice, veggies and shrimp are well blended. Let the rice rest for at least 45 seconds so that the pan reheats. Toss again.

Add the beaten egg and toss until the egg is cooked through. Serve.

"Talk does not cook rice."
Chinese Proverb

The refrigerator light goes on...
This is one of those recipes that you can use the basic structure and build what you want. After the rice is cooked the rest is pretty much up to you. Green onions are a good choice instead of onions. You could use edamame instead of peas. Instead of the shrimp, diced pork tenderloin or chicken thighs work great. You can add cilantro or parsley at the end if you want. This is fried rice, and by its very nature a dish made from leftovers.

Nutrition Facts	
Serving size	about 2 1/2 Cups rice
Servings	2
Calories 434	Calories from Fat 90
	% Daily Value
Total Fat 10 g	16 %
Saturated Fat 2 g	10 %
Trans Fat 0 g	
Monounsaturated Fat 4 g	
Cholesterol 233 mg	78 %
Sodium 490 mg	20 %
Total Carbohydrates 57 g	19 %
Dietary Fiber 7 g	28 %
Sugars 9 g	
Protein 28 g	
Vitamin A 214 %	Vitamin C 33 %
Calcium 13 %	Iron 25 %
Vitamin K 30 mcg	
Potassium 744 mg	
Magnesium 133 mg	

Sloppy Joes

4 **30 min.**

Serving size = about 1 1/2 Cups Sloppy Joe on a bun

This recipe can easily be multiplied or halved. Leftovers are great. Reheat gently.

Served with Mashed Yams or Roasted Corn on the Cob (recipes included).

1 tsp.	olive oil
1 large	onion (diced)
1	rib celery (diced)
1 large	carrot (peeled and diced)
1 small	green bell pepper (diced)
1 lb.	97% lean ground beef
1 Tbsp.	red wine vinegar
1 Tbsp.	Worcestershire sauce
1/2 tsp.	paprika
2 Tbsp.	tomato paste
to taste	fresh ground black pepper
1 1/2 Cups	water
4	whole wheat hamburger buns or Kaiser rolls

Place the olive oil in a large skillet over medium-high heat. Add the onion, celery, carrot and bell pepper. Cook for about 5 minutes stirring occasionally.

Add the ground beef and cook, stirring frequently, until it is browned.

Add the vinegar, Worcestershire, paprika, tomato paste, pepper and water. Reduce the heat to medium low and simmer for about 20 minutes stirring occasionally.

Serve over lightly toasted hamburger buns.

"Sacred cows make the best hamburger."
Mark Twain, Author

The refrigerator light goes on...
I love Sloppy Joes. It's one of those comfort foods that's cheap, easy to make and it can be really good for you. Choose lean ground beef, fresh veggies and these simple spices rather than getting your Sloppy Joe out of a can or a seasoning packet. Lower in fat and salt, with a fresh homemade taste, this recipe won't take much longer than the "instant" mixes.

Nutrition Facts	
Serving size	1 1/2 C. Sloppy Joe/bun
Servings	4
Calories 340	Calories from Fat 71
	% Daily Value
Total Fat 8 g	12 %
Saturated Fat 3 g	15 %
Trans Fat 0 g	
Monounsaturated Fat 3 g	
Cholesterol 69 mg	23 %
Sodium 453 mg	19 %
Total Carbohydrates 39 g	13 %
Dietary Fiber 7 g	26 %
Sugars 12 g	
Protein 30 g	
Vitamin A 68 %	Vitamin C 46 %
Calcium 11 %	Iron 27 %
Vitamin K 10 mcg	
Potassium 944 mg	
Magnesium 83 mg	

Stuffed Creole Chicken

4 **60 min.**

Serving size = 1 stuffed chicken thigh

This recipe can easily be multiplied or halved and makes great leftovers.

Serve with Kale with Nutmeg and Honey and Oregano Rice (recipes included).

2 tsp.	olive oil
8 ounces	mushrooms
1 large	shallot (minced)
1/4 large	green bell pepper (diced)
1	rib celery (diced)
1/4 tsp.	salt
to taste	fresh ground black pepper
2 tsp.	no salt added Creole seasoning (divided)
2 ounces	reduced fat cream cheese
4	boneless skinless chicken thighs
	spray oil

Place 1 teaspoon of olive oil in a large skillet over medium high heat. Add the sliced mushroom and cook, tossing frequently, until well caramelized. Set aside on a plate.

Place the remaining teaspoon olive oil in the skillet. Add the shallot, green pepper and celery. Cook, tossing frequently, for about 10 minutes.

Add the salt, pepper, 1 1/2 teaspoons of the Creole seasoning and the cooked mushrooms. Cook for about 2 minutes and place in a bowl to cool.

Preheat the oven to 350°F.

While the mix is cooling, place each piece of chicken on a sheet of plastic wrap. Fold the wrap over to cover the chicken. Using a meat mallet or the back of a small sauce pan, pound the thighs until they flatten. Start in the center and work outward until the chicken has about doubled in size.

When the vegetables have cooled slightly, add the cream cheese and fold together until well blended.

Divide the vegetable stuffing into 4 portions. Place each portion on a flattened chicken thigh and roll

the thigh tightly around the stuffing. Roll the plastic wrap around the rolled up chicken thigh and twist the ends, spinning the center like the wrapping around a Tootsie Roll. Place the rolled up chicken thighs in the freezer for about 20 minutes.

Spray the pan in the oven lightly with oil. Unwrap the chicken thighs and place them in the pan. Sprinkle with the other 1/2 teaspoon Creole Seasoning. Roast for about 20 minutes, turning about three times until browned on each side. Serve.

"Creole is New Orleans city food. Communities were created by the people who wanted to stay and not go back to Spain or France."
Paul Prudhomme, Chef

The refrigerator light goes on...
Stuffed chicken recipes like this one are a lot easier than you think. The key is to pound the chicken just right. I have a meat mallet but you can use the back of a sauce pan. Start with the thickest part of the meat and pound lightly, working your way toward the outside.

Nutrition Facts	
Serving size	1 stuffed chicken thigh
Servings	4
Calories 179	Calories from Fat 72
	% Daily Value
Total Fat 8 g	12 %
Saturated Fat 2 g	12 %
Trans Fat 0 g	
Monounsaturated Fat 3 g	
Cholesterol 77 mg	26 %
Sodium 297 mg	12 %
Total Carbohydrates 8 g	3 %
Dietary Fiber 1 g	5 %
Sugars 2 g	
Protein 20 g	
Vitamin A 12 %	Vitamin C 33 %
Calcium 5 %	Iron 10 %
Vitamin K 9 mcg	
Potassium 534 mg	
Magnesium 35 mg	

Tuscan Meatloaf

6 **120 min.**

Serving size = 1/6 meatloaf with beans and sauce

This recipe keeps well for about 48 hours in the fridge after being cooked. Great as sandwiches, whether cold or reheated.

2 15-ounce cans	no salt added white beans (drained and rinsed)
2 tsp.	dried oregano
1 tsp.	rubbed sage
1 tsp.	paprika
1 tsp.	ground fennel seed
4 cloves	garlic (finely minced)
1/2 tsp.	salt
1/8 tsp.	fresh ground black pepper
1 1/2 lbs.	extra lean ground beef
2 Tbsp.	olive oil
1 small	onion (diced)
2	ribs celery (diced)
1 medium	carrot (peeled and diced)
1 15-ounce can	no salt added diced tomatoes (undrained)
8 large	black olives (thinly sliced)
1/4 Cup	water

Preheat oven to 325°F.

Mash 1/2 can of the beans together with the oregano, paprika, fennel, 3 cloves of the garlic, salt and pepper.

Mix the ground beef together with the mashed beans until well blended. Fold in the other 1/2 can of beans.

Roll the mixture into a large ball and then shape into a loaf. Place the loaf in the refrigerator.

Place the olive oil in a large skillet over medium heat. Add the garlic and cook for about 3 minutes. Add the onions, celery and carrot and cook for about 5 minutes. Add the diced tomatoes, stir and add the second can of white beans and sliced olives and the water.

Place the meatloaf in the pan surrounded by the vegetable and bean mixture.

Place the pan in the oven. Cook for about 90 minutes, basting the top occasionally with the tomato sauce from the pan. Cook until the internal temperature is 150°F. Remove from the oven and let rest for about 5 – 10 minutes before slicing.

"If you're a lover of food you need to make love to that plate cause it's waitin' on ya."
Mekiel Ruben, Musician

The refrigerator light goes on...
Meatloaf is fantastic because you can make it on a Sunday in about 20 minutes prep time. The great thing is that you'll have leftovers for the week. This is a great variation on meatloaf with everything in one pan – protein, great carbs and veggies all wrapped up in good fats and great Tuscan seasoning. Serve this with a great side salad and you are set.

Nutrition Facts	
Serving size 1/6 loaf w/beans & sauce	
Servings	6
Calories 357	Calories from Fat 104
	% Daily Value
Total Fat 12 g	18 %
Saturated Fat 3 g	17 %
Trans Fat 0 g	
Monounsaturated Fat 5 g	
Cholesterol 30 mg	10 %
Sodium 344 mg	14 %
Total Carbohydrates 17 g	6 %
Dietary Fiber 11 g	45 %
Sugars 3 g	
Protein 38 g	
Vitamin A 41 %	Vitamin C 15 %
Calcium 13 %	Iron 36 %
Vitamin K 12 mcg	
Potassium 1031 mg	
Magnesium 100 mg	

Whitefish in Foil with Vegetables and Tomato Sauce

2 **30 min.**

Serving size = 4 ounces fish with vegetables and sauce

This recipe can easily be multiplied or halved but does not keep well.

4	spears asparagus
1 15-ounce can	no salt added white beans (drained and rinsed)
2 4-ounce	halibut filets
1 small	carrot (cut matchstick)
1/4 small	green bell pepper (cut matchstick)
1/4 small	red bell pepper (cut matchstick)
4 medium	crimini mushrooms (sliced)
4 large	basil leaves
4 tsp.	tomato paste
1/4 Cup	dry white wine
4 tsp.	extra virgin olive oil
1/4 tsp.	salt
fresh ground black pepper (to taste)	
2	sheets aluminum foil

Slice the asparagus lengthwise and then cut the spears into quarters (each spear will end up with eight pieces).

Preheat the oven to 400°F.

Fold the foil so that it is almost a square (15 inches x 12 inches). Starting at one end of the folded edge, cut a half of a heart shape in such a way that when the parchment is opened it is in the shape of a heart.

Place half of the beans on each parchment paper.

Rinse the halibut filets in cold water and pat dry. Put filets on top of the beans. Center the filets on one side of the cut heart so that the other side will fold over the top of the filets easily.

Sprinkle 1/8 tsp. of the salt over each of the pairs of sole filets. Add fresh pepper to taste.

Scatter the carrots, red and green peppers, sliced mushrooms and asparagus over the fish evenly.

Mix together the tomato paste and wine. Pour the mixture over the filets. Drizzle the top of the filets with the olive oil.

Close the foil paper by rolling the edge inward, starting at the point of the heart and working around to the base of the heart. The foil pouch with the fish inside will be in the shape of a large half circle.

Place the pouches on a cookie sheet and then into the oven. Reduce the heat to 375°F and cook for 15 minutes.

Remove each pouch to a plate and let stand 30 seconds before cutting the pouch open. There will be some hot steam that escapes when the parchment is cut (be careful!).

The refrigerator light goes on...
This is a fantastic way to cook fish. It is traditionally baked in parchment paper but for most folks the foil is more practical. You can use almost any combination of fish filet, vegetables, liquid and herb or spice along with the olive oil.

Nutrition Facts	
Serving size	4 oz. fish w/ veggies
Servings	2
Calories 430	Calories from Fat 133
	% Daily Value
Total Fat 15 g	19 %
Saturated Fat 2 g	7 %
Trans Fat 0 g	
Monounsaturated Fat 3 g	
Cholesterol 36 mg	12 %
Sodium 388 mg	18 %
Total Carbohydrates 40 g	12 %
Dietary Fiber 12 g	39 %
Sugars 4 g	
Protein 38 g	
Vitamin A 108 %	Vitamin C 63 %
Calcium 15 %	Iron 29 %
Vitamin K 47 mcg	
Potassium 1552 mg	
Magnesium 1920 mg	

Baked Sweet Potato

Servings = 1
Serving size = 1 6-ounce yam

This recipe is easily multiplied but does not make very good leftovers.

1	6-ounce yam
1 tsp.	unsalted butter
1/2 ounce	goat cheese
	sprinkle salt

Wash the yam well.

Place the yam on a sheet of aluminum foil and place in the oven. Set the temperature to 325°F.

Bake the potato for about 40 minutes until it is soft. You'll know because it will give slightly when squeezed.

Serve with the butter and goat cheese. Sprinkle just a tiny bit of salt over the top.

"We must eat to live and live to eat."
Henry Fielding, Playwright

The refrigerator light goes on...
More and more yams are being sold in America as yams. For the longest time they would be labeled "sweet potatoes." Actual sweet potatoes are not widely available.

So why not call this recipe "Baked Yam?" I don't know. Baked Sweet Potato just sounds better.

Nutrition Facts	
Serving size	1 6-ounce yam
Servings	1
Calories 273	Calories from Fat 64
	% Daily Value
Total Fat 7 g	11 %
Saturated Fat 4 g	19 %
Trans Fat 0 g	
Monounsaturated Fat 2 g	
Cholesterol 17 mg	5 %
Sodium 213 mg	8 %
Total Carbohydrates 47 g	18 %
Dietary Fiber 7 g	24 %
Sugars 1 g	
Protein 6 g	
Vitamin A 11 %	Vitamin C 48 %
Calcium 2 %	Iron 8 %
Vitamin K 4 mcg	
Potassium 1393 mg	
Magnesium 38 mg	

Coconut Rice

Servings = 2
Serving size = 1/2 Cup cooked rice

This recipe can easily be multiplied but does not make very good leftovers.

1/2 cup	reduced-fat (lite) unsweetened coconut milk
3/4 cup	water
1/8 tsp.	salt
1/2 cup	jasmine rice

Prior to opening the can of coconut milk, shake very well.

In a medium sauce pain, heat the coconut milk, water and salt. When the liquid boils, stir in the jasmine rice.

Reduce heat to medium-low and simmer, covered, for about 15 minutes.

Do not boil away all of the liquid and do not stir the rice.

When a very small amount of liquid remains, remove the pan from the burner and let it stand, covered, for 5 minutes before serving.

"Rice is a beautiful food. It is beautiful when it grows, precision rows of sparkling green stalks shooting up to reach the hot summer sun. It is beautiful when harvested, autumn gold sheaves piled on diked, patchwork paddies. It is beautiful when, once threshed, it enters granary bins like a (flood) of tiny seed-pearls. It is beautiful when cooked by a practiced hand, pure white and sweetly fragrant."

Shizuo Tsuji, Japanese
chef and cookbook author

The refrigerator light goes on...
Never stir rice. It doesn't matter how you cook it, stirring it breaks down the starches on the outer layer and turns the rice to a gooey paste. Simply place the rice in the boiling liquid, stir once and cover. Leave it alone until the water is evaporated.

Nutrition Facts	
Serving size	1/2 Cup cooked rice
Servings	2
Calories 211	Calories from Fat 35
	% Daily Value
Total Fat 4 g	6 %
Saturated Fat 3 g	14 %
Trans Fat 0 g	
Monounsaturated Fat 0 g	
Cholesterol 0 mg	0 %
Sodium 153 mg	7 %
Total Carbohydrates 38 g	13 %
Dietary Fiber 1 g	2 %
Sugars 1 g	
Protein 3 g	
Vitamin A 0 %	Vitamin C 0 %
Calcium 2 %	Iron 12 %
Vitamin K 0 mcg	
Potassium 53 mg	
Magnesium 12 mg	

Creamed Spinach

Servings = 2
Serving size = about 1 Cup

This recipe can easily be multiplied and makes OK
leftovers. Reheat gently.

1	10-ounce package frozen spinach (thawed)
1 tsp.	olive oil
1/2 small	onion (diced)
1/4 Cup	2% milk
1 ounce	reduced fat cream cheese (cut into small chunks for easier melting)
to taste	fresh ground black pepper
1/8 tsp.	ground nutmeg

Place the spinach in a strainer and press with a rubber
spatula or spoon until all excess water is removed.

Place the olive oil in a skillet over medium heat. Add
the diced onion and cook about 5 minutes until softened.

Add the spinach and cook for about 2 minutes. Add
the milk, cream cheese, pepper and nutmeg.

Cook until the cheese is melted and well blended into
the spinach. Serve.

*"Food, like a loving touch or a glimpse of divine
power, has that ability to comfort."*
Norman Kolpas, Author

The refrigerator light goes on...
Even when you don't like spinach, creamed
spinach is good. To me it's great comfort
food. The bitterness that you might not like
about cooked spinach is balanced well with the
creaminess of the cheese, and the nutmeg adds
just the right touch of aromatic spice.

Nutrition Facts	
Serving size	about 1 Cup
Servings	2
Calories 75	Calories from Fat 28
	% Daily Value
Total Fat 5 g	8 %
Saturated Fat 3 g	2 %
Trans Fat 0 g	
Monounsaturated Fat 2 g	
Cholesterol 1 mg	0 %
Sodium 156 mg	7 %
Total Carbohydrates 8 g	3 %
Dietary Fiber 4 g	18 %
Sugars 2 g	
Protein 6 g	
Vitamin A 333 %	Vitamin C 15 %
Calcium 21 %	Iron 15 %
Vitamin K 530 mcg	
Potassium 532 mg	
Magnesium 110 mg	

Ginger Snow Peas

Servings = 2
Serving size = 4 ounces snow peas

This recipe can easily be multiplied and leftovers are good chilled.

2 tsp.	sesame oil
1 tsp.	fresh ginger (peeled and minced)
1 small	shallot (minced)
8 ounces	snow peas
2 tsp.	low sodium soy sauce
to taste	fresh ground black pepper

Place the sesame oil in a small skillet over medium heat. Add the ginger and shallot.

Cook for about 4 minutes stirring frequently.

Add the snow peas, soy sauce and pepper. Toss well.

Cover and cook for about 8 to 12 minutes, tossing frequently, until soft.

Serve.

"He who eats with most pleasure is he who least requires sauce."

Xenophon, Greek soldier

The refrigerator light goes on...
This simple side dish goes well with any Asian meal.

Nutrition Facts	
Serving size	4 oz. snow peas
Servings	2
Calories 112	Calories from Fat 43
	% Daily Value
Total Fat 5 g	7 %
Saturated Fat 1 g	3 %
Trans Fat 0 g	
Monounsaturated Fat 2 g	
Cholesterol 0 mg	0 %
Sodium 185 mg	7 %
Total Carbohydrates 14 g	6 %
Dietary Fiber 3 g	8 %
Sugars 5 g	
Protein 4 g	
Vitamin A 30 %	Vitamin C 116 %
Calcium 5 %	Iron 15 %
Vitamin K 29 mcg	
Potassium 336 mg	
Magnesium 35 mg	

Herbed Zucchini

Servings = 4
Serving size = about 2/3 Cup

This recipe can easily be multipled but does not make very good leftovers.

1 Tbsp.	olive oil
1 lb.	zucchini (1/2 inch dice)
2 Tbsp.	fresh herbs of your choice
1/4 tsp.	salt
to taste	fresh ground black pepper

Place the olive oil in a large non-stick skillet over medium-high heat. When the oil is hot add the zucchini. Let the zucchini cook without stirring for about 3 minutes. If it appears to be cooking too fast, reduce the heat to medium.

Toss the zucchini well and cook for about 7 - 10 more minutes. As the cubes begin to brown add the herbs, salt and pepper and continue to toss.

Do not over cook the zucchini. As soon as the outside is lightly browned and it is slightly soft serve.

"If one consults enough herbals... every sickness known to humanity will be listed as being cured by sage."

Varro Taylor, Ph.D., Pharmacologist

The refrigerator light goes on...
The choice of herbs here is not important. Use what you have in the garden or the fridge. Equal amounts of basil, chive, sage, rosemary and oregano will do but you could just as easily choose thyme, sage, marjoram and tarragon. This recipe will work with dried herbs but it just isn't quite as good somehow.

Nutrition Facts	
Serving size	about 2/3 Cup
Servings	4
Calories 51	Calories from Fat 32
	% Daily Value
Total Fat 4 g	6 %
Saturated Fat 1 g	3 %
Trans Fat 0 g	
Monounsaturated Fat 3 g	
Cholesterol 0 mg	0 %
Sodium 88 mg	4 %
Total Carbohydrates 5 g	2 %
Dietary Fiber 2 g	7 %
Sugars 2 g	
Protein 2 g	
Vitamin A 6 %	Vitamin C 33 %
Calcium 4 %	Iron 8 %
Vitamin K 26 mcg	
Potassium 321 mg	
Magnesium 23 mg	

Jasmine Rice

Servings = 2
Serving size = 1/2 cup cooked rice

This recipe can easily be multiplied but does not keep well.

1 1/2 Cups	water
1/8 tsp.	salt
1/2 Cup	jasmine rice

In a medium sauce pan, heat the water and salt. When the water boils, stir in the jasmine rice.

Reduce heat to medium-low and simmer, partially covered, for about 15 minutes.

Do not boil away all of the liquid and do not stir the rice.

When a very small amount of liquid remains, remove the pan from the burner and let it stand, covered, for 5 minutes before serving.

Combine the cooked carrots with the light spread, maple syrup and salt and serve.

"Rice is the best, the most nutritive and unquestionably the most widespread staple in the world."

Auguste Escoffier, 19th century French chef

The refrigerator light goes on...
Simple, simple, simple.... When you add rice and salt to water and simmer and you don't stir the result is perfect.

Nutrition Facts	
Serving size	1/2 Cup cooked rice
Servings	2
Calories 169	Calories from Fat 0
	% Daily Value
Total Fat 0 g	0 %
Saturated Fat 0 g	0 %
Trans Fat 0 g	
Monounsaturated Fat 0 g	
Cholesterol 0 mg	0 %
Sodium 142 mg	5 %
Total Carbohydrates 37 g	12 %
Dietary Fiber 1 g	2 %
Sugars 0 g	
Protein 3 g	
Vitamin A 0 %	Vitamin C 0 %
Calcium 1 %	Iron 11 %
Vitamin K 0 mcg	
Potassium 53 mg	
Magnesium 13 mg	

Kale with Nutmeg and Honey

Servings = 2
Serving size = 4 ounces kale

This recipe can be multiplied by 2. Leftovers keep
well and make a good addition to sandwiches, salads
and egg dishes.

1 tsp.	olive oil
8 ounces	fresh kale (thinly sliced crosswise)
2 tsp.	honey
1/4 tsp.	ground nutmeg
1/8 tsp.	salt
fresh ground black pepper (to taste)	

Heat oil over high heat in a large non-stick skillet.
Add the kale and cook, tossing frequently.

As it begins to wilt, add the honey, nutmeg, salt and
pepper.

Cook until the kale is very hot, stirring frequently.

When the kale is wilted, but still bright green, it is
done. This should take only about 2 minutes.

*"Kale is a leafy vegetable that is bold and bitter,
but it's packed with vitamins and minerals. You
can juice it like you would carrots, putting whole
stalks into a vegetable drink. It'll boost your greens
and your energy levels."*

Chi Lang, Chef

The refrigerator light goes on...
One of the great things about kale is that it cooks
so quickly and you can use almost any flavors with
it – honey, maple syrup, olive oil, sesame oil, spicy
flavors or sweet ones.

Nutrition Facts	
Serving size	4 ounces kale
Servings	2
Calories 99	Calories from Fat 27
	% Daily Value
Total Fat 3 g	5 %
Saturated Fat 0 g	2 %
Trans Fat 0 g	
Monounsaturated Fat 2 g	
Cholesterol 0 mg	0 %
Sodium 194 mg	8 %
Total Carbohydrates 17 g	6 %
Dietary Fiber 2 g	9 %
Sugars 15 g	
Protein 11 g	
Vitamin A 344 %	Vitamin C 224 %
Calcium 12 %	Iron 18 %
Vitamin K 917 mcg	
Potassium 505 mg	
Magnesium 39 mg	

Maple Sage Carrots

Servings = 2
Serving size = 1/2 cup rice

This recipe can easily be multiplied and makes great leftovers.

1 quart	water
2 lb.	baby carrots
2 tsp.	unsalted butter
2 tsp.	olive oil
3 tsp.	dried sage
1/4 tsp.	salt
to taste	fresh ground black pepper
2 Tbsp.	pure maple syrup

Place the water in a medium pot fitted with a steamer basket over high heat. Add the carrots and steam for about 10 minutes.

Steam for about 10 minutes.

Place the butter and olive oil in a large non-stick skillet over medium high heat. Add the carrots and cook, tossing frequently. After the carrots begin to turn slightly brown, lower the heat to medium.

Toss and add the sage, salt and pepper. Cook for about 2 minutes. Add the maple syrup, toss and cook for about 1 minute. Serve.

"Bad cooks - and the utter lack of reason in the kitchen - have delayed human development longest and impaired it most."

Fredrich Nietzche,
Philosopher

The refrigerator light goes on...
The little baby carrots are not really baby carrots. They're grown up carrots that are cut to look like baby carrots. They are a little more expensive, but it makes it easier because you don't have to prep them.

Nutrition Facts	
Serving size	about 1 Cup
Servings	3
Calories 103	Calories from Fat 28
	% Daily Value
Total Fat 3 g	5 %
Saturated Fat 1 g	5 %
Trans Fat 0 g	
Monounsaturated Fat 3 g	
Cholesterol 3 mg	1 %
Sodium 201 mg	8 %
Total Carbohydrates 19 g	6 %
Dietary Fiber 4 g	17 %
Sugars 11 g	
Protein 1 g	
Vitamin A 500 %	Vitamin C 15 %
Calcium 6 %	Iron 3 %
Vitamin K 24 mcg	
Potassium 494 mg	
Magnesium 20 mg	

Mashed Yams

Servings = 4
Serving size = about 1 Cup

This recipe can easily be multiplied and will keep well, refrigerated, about 48 hours. Reheat gently.

1 quart	water
1 lb.	yams (peeled and cubed)
1 tsp.	extra virgin olive oil
1 large	shallot (minced)
1/4 tsp.	dried rosemary
1/4 tsp.	salt
to taste	fresh ground black pepper
2 Tbsp.	light spread (like Promise Buttery Spread Light or Smart Balance Light)
1/4 Cup	non-fat buttermilk
2 Tbsp.	2% milk

Place the water in a large stock pot fitted with a steamer basket over high heat.

Add the cubed yams to the steamer basket and steam until they break slightly with a fork.

While the yams are cooking, place the olive oil in a small skillet over medium heat. Add the shallots and rosemary and cook gently until the shallots are softened.

Place the cooked yams together with the shallot and rosemary mixture in a bowl. Add the salt, pepper, spread and buttermilk and mash with a fork until smooth. Add the 2% milk slowly as the yams are mashed smooth.

The mashed yams can be reheated gently in a microwave.

"Strange to see how a good dinner and feasting reconciles everybody."

Samuel Pepys, Culinarian

The refrigerator light goes on...
This is the perfect recipe to substitute for mashed potatoes. The same creamy mashed potato dish that's so comforting with the twist of added flavor. And the added benefit of more fiber!

Nutrition Facts	
Serving size	about 1 Cup
Servings	4
Calories 188	Calories from Fat 37
	% Daily Value
Total Fat 4 g	6 %
Saturated Fat 1 g	5 %
Trans Fat 0 g	
Monounsaturated Fat 2 g	
Cholesterol 1 mg	0 %
Sodium 215 mg	9 %
Total Carbohydrates 35 g	12 %
Dietary Fiber 5 g	19 %
Sugars 2 g	
Protein 3 g	
Vitamin A 14 %	Vitamin C 35 %
Calcium 6 %	Iron 4 %
Vitamin K 6 mcg	
Potassium 1021 mg	
Magnesium 31 mg	

Mustard Vinaigrette Green Beans

Servings = 3
Serving size = about 1 Cup

This recipe can easily be multiplied and makes good leftovers. Reheat gently so they don't get mushy. The beans will lose their bright color and look a little grayish - this is normal.

1 quart	water
12 ounces	fresh whole green beans
2 tsp.	olive oil
1 tsp.	balsamic vinegar
2 tsp.	Dijon mustard
2 tsp.	water
1/4 tsp.	salt
to taste	fresh ground black pepper
1/8 tsp.	dried tarragon

Place the water in a medium pot fitted with a steamer basket over high heat.

Add the green beans and cover. Cook for about 10 minutes until tender.

While the beans are cooking, place the olive oil, vinegar, mustard, water, salt, pepper and tarragon in a medium mixing bowl. Whisk until smooth.

When the beans are tender, add them to the dressing. Toss to coat well. Serve.

"Love is like a mustard seed; planted by God and watered by men."

Muda Saint Michael, Poet

The refrigerator light goes on...
There might be an argument for using a pound of beans for the amount of dressing, but I wanted to make sure that there was no feeling of any skimping on the sauce. There's enough to make this simple side dish rich and tasty. When I asked my wife to taste these she said, "Wow, that's the stuff." We both had to tear ourselves away from the bowl (not that it matters all that much since there are almost no calories).

Nutrition Facts	
Serving size	about 1 Cup
Servings	3
Calories 64	Calories from Fat 29
	% Daily Value
Total Fat 3 g	5 %
Saturated Fat 0 g	2 %
Trans Fat 0 g	
Monounsaturated Fat 2 g	
Cholesterol 0 mg	0 %
Sodium 239 mg	10 %
Total Carbohydrates 8 g	3 %
Dietary Fiber 4 g	16 %
Sugars 2 g	
Protein 2 g	
Vitamin A 16 %	Vitamin C 31 %
Calcium 4 %	Iron 7 %
Vitamin K 18 mcg	
Potassium 240 mg	
Magnesium 30 mg	

Oregano Rice

Servings = 4
Serving size = about 1 Cup

This recipe can be easily halved or multiplied. It keep well and is also good chilled.

2 1/4 cups	water
1/4 tsp	salt
1/2 cup	long grain brown rice
1 small	shallot (minced)
2 tsp	extra virgin olive oil
1 Tbsp	fresh oregano

In a medium sauce pan, heat the water and salt. When the water boils, stir in the brown rice.

Reduce heat to medium-low and simmer, partially covered, for about 15 minutes.

Do not boil away all of the liquid and do not stir the rice.

When a very small amount of liquid remains, remove the pan from the burner and add the shallot, olive oil and oregano. Toss well and cover. Let stand for about 5 minutes, then serve.

"Let food be thy medicine and medicine be thy food."

Hippocrates, Philosopher

The refrigerator light goes on...
By mincing the shallot very finely and adding it to the rice while it sits and continues to steam, it will actually cook slightly. Combined with the olive oil and oregano, this makes for a fragrant and simple side dish.

Nutrition Facts	
Serving size	1/2 Cup cooked rice
Servings	2
Calories 221	Calories from Fat 52
	% Daily Value
Total Fat 6 g	9 %
Saturated Fat 1 g	3 %
Trans Fat 0 g	
Monounsaturated Fat 0 g	
Cholesterol 0 mg	0 %
Sodium 294 mg	12 %
Total Carbohydrates 38 g	13 %
Dietary Fiber 2 g	6 %
Sugars 0 g	
Protein 4 g	
Vitamin A 3 %	Vitamin C 2 %
Calcium 3 %	Iron 7 %
Vitamin K 6 mcg	
Potassium 168 mg	
Magnesium 71 mg	

Orzo with Tapenade

Servings = 2
Serving size = 2 ounces orzo

This recipe can easily be multiplied but does not make good leftovers.

3 quarts	water
4 ounces	orzo pasta
1 tsp.	olive oil
1 large	shallot (sliced)
1 Tbsp.	capers
1/4	red bell pepper (diced)
1 Tbsp.	tapenade
to taste	fresh ground black pepper

Place the water in a medium stock pot over high heat. When the water boils add the orzo. Cook for about ten minutes until the pasta is cooked al dente.

While the orzo is cooking place a medium skillet on the range over medium heat. Add the olive oil, shallots and capers. Cook gently for about 5 - 7 minutes.

Add the red pepper and olives and cook until the pasta is done.

Drain the pasta and add it to the skillet. Add the tepanade and the pepper and cook for about two minutes until well blended.

"It's diamonds in your pockets one week, macaroni and cheese the next."

Graham Kerr, Genius

The refrigerator light goes on...
Well, for me it's macaroni one week and macaroni the next without the diamonds in my pocket. But I do love pasta, especially this perfect Mediterranean side dish to serve with grilled fish, chicken or pork. The flavor of the tapenade is great and you can buy it easily in most grocery stores. The jar might say "olive oil spread" or something like "kalamata olive spread." The saltiness along with the umami flavor of the tapenade makes the perfect way to flavor the orzo.

Nutrition Facts	
Serving size	2 ounces orzo
Servings	2
Calories 276	Calories from Fat 46
	% Daily Value
Total Fat 5 g	8 %
Saturated Fat 1 g	4 %
Trans Fat 0 g	
Monounsaturated Fat 3 g	
Cholesterol 0 mg	0 %
Sodium 258 mg	11 %
Total Carbohydrates 49 g	16 %
Dietary Fiber 3 g	11 %
Sugars 2 g	
Protein 8 g	
Vitamin A 19 %	Vitamin C 44 %
Calcium 4 %	Iron 15 %
Vitamin K 4 mcg	
Potassium 261 mg	
Magnesium 40 mg	

Pan Grilled Asparagus

Servings = 4
Serving size = 4 ounces asparagus

This recipe can easily be multiplied and will keep fairly well if chilled immediately.

1 quart	water
8 ounces	asparagus spears
1 tsp.	water
	spray olive oil
1/8 tsp.	salt
2 quarts	ice water

Cut the woody ends off the base of the asparagus spears.

Heat 1 quart of water in a shallow pan over medium-high heat. The water should never come to a full boil.

Place the asparagus in the water and cook for about 5 – 7 minutes until the spears begin to lose their firmness.

Remove and place the ice water. When the asparagus is cooled, remove it from the water and drain.

Place a large non-stick skillet (or roasting pan) in the oven and preheat to 400°F. When the pan is hot, add the asparagus, spray lightly with olive oil and sprinkle the salt over the top. Cook for about 5 minutes and toss the asparagus to coat well. Make sure that all sides come in contact with the pan. They will take 10 to 15 minutes total cooking time and should be tossed every 3 – 5 minutes.

"Pray how does your asparagus perform?"
John Adams, second President of the United States, writing to his wife Abigail Adams

The refrigerator light goes on...
Pan grilled veggies are quick and easy. They are great for you and have almost no calories. If you don't like asparagus, try pan-grilled broccoli or leeks.

Nutrition Facts	
Serving size	4 ounces asparagus
Servings	2
Calories 23	Calories from Fat 0
	% Daily Value
Total Fat 0 g	0 %
Saturated Fat 0 g	0 %
Trans Fat 0 g	
Monounsaturated Fat 0 g	
Cholesterol 0 mg	0 %
Sodium 153 mg	6 %
Total Carbohydrates 4 g	1 %
Dietary Fiber 2 g	10 %
Sugars 2 g	
Protein 3 g	
Vitamin A 17 %	Vitamin C 11 %
Calcium 3 %	Iron 14 %
Vitamin K 47 mcg	
Potassium 230 mg	
Magnesium 16 mg	

Pan Grilled Broccoli

Servings = 2
Serving size = 4 ounces broccoli

This recipe can easily be multiplied and will keep fairly well if chilled immediately.

2	medium beets
1 tsp.	unsalted butter
1/4 tsp.	salt
1/8 tsp.	dried oregano
1/8 tsp.	chili powder

Preheat the oven to 400°F.

Trim the bottom inch of the stem from the broccoli. Using a vegetable peeler, peel the tough outer layer from the stems.

Heat 1 quart of water in a large sauce pan or stock pot fitted with a steamer basket over high heat. When the water is boiling, add the broccoli to the steamer and cook for about 12 - 15 minutes until the spears begin to lose their firmness.

Remove and plunge into the ice water. When the broccoli spears are cooled, remove from the water and drain.

Place a large non-stick skillet (or roasting pan) in the oven and preheat to 400°F. When the pan is hot, add the broccoli, spray lightly with olive oil and sprinkle the salt over the top. Cook for about 5 minutes and turn to sear well. Make sure that all of the spears come in contact with the pan. They will take 15 to 20 minutes total cooking time and should be turned every 3 – 5 minutes.

"The greatest delight the fields and woods minister is the suggestion of an occult relation between man and the vegetable. 'I am not alone and unacknowledged.' They nod to me and I to them."
Ralph Waldo Emerson, Poet

The refrigerator light goes on...
Pre-cooked veggies, added to a smoking hot pan with just a bit of oil, will sear and crisp the outside and add a fresh roasted flavor.

Nutrition Facts	
Serving size	4 ounces broccoli
Servings	2
Calories 39	Calories from Fat 4
	% Daily Value
Total Fat 0 g	1 %
Saturated Fat 0 g	0 %
Trans Fat 0 g	
Monounsaturated Fat 0 g	
Cholesterol 0 mg	0 %
Sodium 44 mg	2 %
Total Carbohydrates 8 g	3 %
Dietary Fiber 3 g	12 %
Sugars 2 g	
Protein 2 g	
Vitamin A 14 %	Vitamin C 169 %
Calcium 5 %	Iron 5 %
Vitamin K 116 mcg	
Potassium 360 mg	
Magnesium 24 mg	

Parmesan Squash

Servings = 2
Serving size = 1 large squash

This recipe can be easily multiplied but does not make very good leftovers.

2	8-ounce yellow squash
2 lbs.	water
to taste	fresh ground black pepper
2 Tbsp.	fresh herbs of your choice
1 ounce	Parmigiano-Reggiano

Place the water in a medium pot fitted with a steamer basket over high heat.

Preheat the oven to 325°F.

Cut about 1/4 inch from the stem end of the squash and then slice lengthwise. Place the four halves in the steamer and steam until slightly tender.

Remove the steamed squash and place in a shallow baking dish. Place the dish in the oven and cook for about 10 minutes. Remove and sprinkle with pepper, fresh herbs and equal amounts of Parmigiano-reggiano.

Return the pan to the oven and cook until the parmesan is melted (about 5 minutes).

"There's no sauce in the world like hunger."
Miguel de Cervantes, Author

The refrigerator light goes on...
These are two perfect ingredients that make a wonderful dish. The yellow squash tastes like Summer and its own buttery flavor is enhanced by the parmesan. I especially like using just a little bit of rosemary for the herb.

Nutrition Facts	
Serving size	1 large squash
Servings	2
Calories 99	Calories from Fat 37
	% Daily Value
Total Fat 4 g	7 %
Saturated Fat 2 g	10 %
Trans Fat 0 g	
Monounsaturated Fat 1 g	
Cholesterol 10 mg	3 %
Sodium 233 mg	10 %
Total Carbohydrates 10 g	3 %
Dietary Fiber 4 g	17 %
Sugars 0 g	
Protein 7 g	
Vitamin A 8 %	Vitamin C 32 %
Calcium 22 %	Iron 7 %
Vitamin K 0 mcg	
Potassium 497 mg	
Magnesium 54 mg	

Plain Mashed Potatoes

Servings = 4
Serving size = about 1 Cup

This recipe can easily be multiplied but does not keep well.

3 quarts	water
1 lb.	Yukon Gold potatoes
2 tsp.	unsalted butter
1/4 Cup	non-fat buttermilk
1/4 Cup	2% milk
1/8 tsp.	salt
	fresh ground black pepper

Place the water in a large stock pot over high heat.

Quarter the potatoes and add to the stock pot. Cover with water by about an inch. Bring to boil and then reduce heat until the water is simmering.

Cook the potatoes about 15 – 20 minutes until slightly soft in the middle. They should give when squeezed.

Remove from heat and drain water. Add butter, buttermilk, milk and salt. Mash potatoes until creamy. I like to leave some chunks. If you like them smooth be careful because over mashing will result in pasty potatoes. Add ground black pepper to taste.

"One potato, two potato, three potato, four."
Child's rhyme

The refrigerator light goes on...
These potatoes have more butter in them than some of the other "flavored" mashed potato recipes in this book. This is to help enhance the creaminess and the mouthfeel that other flavors like roasted garlic or pesto achieve with less fat.

Nutrition Facts	
Serving size	1 cup
Servings	4
Calories 119	Calories from Fat 21
	% Daily Value
Total Fat 2 g	4 %
Saturated Fat 2 g	8 %
Trans Fat 0 g	
Monounsaturated Fat 0 g	
Cholesterol 7 mg	2 %
Sodium 178 mg	7 %
Total Carbohydrates 21 g	7 %
Dietary Fiber 3 g	10 %
Sugars 2 g	
Protein 3 g	
Vitamin A 1 %	Vitamin C 38 %
Calcium 5 %	Iron 5 %
Vitamin K 2 mcg	
Potassium 532 mg	
Magnesium 30 mg	

Roasted Corn on the Cob

Servings = 2
Serving size = 1 ear corn

This recipe can easily be multiplied. I love leftover corn. Leave it wrapped in the husks inside the foil.

2	ears corn
1/8 tsp	pepper
1/4 tsp	salt
2 tsp	unsalted butter

Preheat the oven to 400°F.

Peel the husk back from the corn, being careful not to detach them from the stem. Remove silks and rinse well, wetting down the husks.

Sprinkle the salt and pepper over the corn.

Fold the husks against the corn and wrap in foil.

Roast in the oven for about 30 minutes. Turn them 1/4 turn about every 7 – 8 minutes.

Remove from the oven and unwrap the foil. Cut the bottom of the cob so that the husks fall away easily.

Serve each with a pat of butter.

These can also be roasted on top of the grill. The heat should be medium to medium-high and you must turn them frequently, as noted above.

"The greatest drawback is the way in which it is necessary to eat it. It looks awkward enough: but what is to be done? Surrendering such a vegetable from considerations of grace is not to be thought of."

Harriet Martineau, an Englishwoman writing about corn on the cob in 1835

The refrigerator light goes on...
This recipe includes the pat of butter for your corn on the cob because it just wouldn't be corn without it. Take the pat and enjoy it. This recipe works well both on the grill and in the oven. The grill will give the corn a lovely charcoal flavor.

Nutrition Facts	
Serving size	1 ear corn
Servings	2
Calories 144	Calories from Fat 44
	% Daily Value
Total Fat 5 g	8 %
Saturated Fat 3 g	13 %
Trans Fat 0 g	
Monounsaturated Fat 1 g	
Cholesterol 10 mg	3 %
Sodium 320 mg	13 %
Total Carbohydrates 26 g	9 %
Dietary Fiber 3 g	11 %
Sugars 4 g	
Protein 3 g	
Vitamin A 2 %	Vitamin C 11 %
Calcium 0 %	Iron 4 %
Vitamin K 1 mcg	
Potassium 258 mg	
Magnesium 33 mg	

Roasted Garlic

Servings = 6
Serving size = 1/3 head of garlic (about 6 cloves)

I make up to about 4 heads of garlic at a time. This keeps well, tightly covered, for about 4 - 6 days.

2	heads whole garlic
2 tsp.	extra virgin olive oil

Preheat oven to 300°F.

Peel the outermost skin of the garlic only. With the bulb whole, turn on its side and slice 1/2-inch of the stem end off the garlic bulbs.

Pour the olive oil in the bottom of a heavy bottom sauce pan.

Place the garlic cut side down in the pan.

Cover and roast for 45 minutes until cloves are slightly brown at the cut end and soft throughout.

"There is no such thing as a little garlic."
Arthur Baer, Investment Author

The refrigerator light goes on...
Roasted garlic is a staple in my kitchen and should be in yours. I generally roast about 3 heads every ten days or so. It makes a great ingredient in mashed potatoes and also enriches any sauce. It is fantastic served as hors d'oeuvres on bread with some soft goat cheese and veggies.

Nutrition Facts	
Serving size	about 6 cloves garlic
Servings	6
Calories 40	Calories from Fat 14
	% Daily Value
Total Fat 2 g	2 %
Saturated Fat 0 g	1 %
Trans Fat 0 g	
Monounsaturated Fat 0 g	
Cholesterol 0 mg	0 %
Sodium 3 mg	0 %
Total Carbohydrates 6 g	2 %
Dietary Fiber <1 g	2 %
Sugars 0 g	
Protein 1 g	
Vitamin A 0 %	Vitamin C 9 %
Calcium 3 %	Iron 2 %
Vitamin K 1 mcg	
Potassium 72 mg	
Magnesium 5 mg	

Roasted Garlic Mashed Potatoes

Servings = 4
Serving size = about 1 Cup

This recipe can easily be multiplied but does not make very good leftovers. This recipe requires making Roasted Garlic (recipe included).

3 quarts	water
1 lb.	Yukon Gold potatoes
2 tsp.	unsalted butter
1/3 Cup	non-fat buttermilk
1/3 Cup	2% milk
1/4 tsp.	salt
4 cloves	roasted garlic

Place the water in a large stock-pot over high heat.

Quarter the potatoes and add them to the stock-pot. Cover with water by about an inch. Bring to boil and then reduce heat until the water is simmering.

Cook the potatoes about 15 – 20 minutes, until slightly soft in the middle. They should give when squeezed.

Remove from heat and drain water. Add butter, buttermilk, milk, salt and roasted garlic. Mash potatoes until creamy and the roasted garlic is well blended. I like to leave some chunks of potatoes. If you like them smooth, be careful because over mashing will result in pasty potatoes.

Add ground black pepper to taste.

"I have made a lot of mistakes falling in love, and regretted most of them, but never the potatoes that went with them."

Nora Ephron, Screenwriter

The refrigerator light goes on...
The key to good mashed potatoes is in the buttermilk / milk combination. The buttermilk adds richness and tartness with no fat, and the milk adds creaminess. The butter is used here only as a flavor enhancer.

Nutrition Facts	
Serving size	about 1 Cup
Servings	4
Calories 130	Calories from Fat 24
	% Daily Value
Total Fat 3 g	4 %
Saturated Fat 2 g	6 %
Trans Fat 0 g	
Monounsaturated Fat 1 g	
Cholesterol 7 mg	2 %
Sodium 100 mg	4 %
Total Carbohydrates 23 g	8 %
Dietary Fiber 3 g	10 %
Sugars 3 g	
Protein 4 g	
Vitamin A 2 %	Vitamin C 40 %
Calcium 7 %	Iron 5 %
Vitamin K 3 mcg	
Potassium 564 mg	
Magnesium 33 mg	

Roasted Root Vegetables

Servings = 4
Serving Size = about 2 Cups vegetables

This recipe can be halved or multiplied and makes good leftovers. Reheat gently.

1 Tbsp.	olive oil
16 ounces	red potatoes (cut into 1 inch cubes)
8 ounces	carrots (peeled and cut into 1 inch pieces)
8 ounces	parsnips (peeled and cut into 1 inch pieces)
8 ounces	shallots (peeled; leave whole)
2 tsp.	dried rosemary
1/4 tsp.	salt
to taste	fresh ground black pepper

Place a large roasting pan in the oven and preheat the oven to 325°F.

When the oven is hot, add the olive oil and swirl to coat the bottom of the pan.

Add the potatoes, carrots, parsnips, shallots, rosemary, salt and pepper. Toss well to coat with the oil.

Roast the vegetables for about 30 to 40 minutes. Stir gently every 10 minutes.

"The feeling of friendship is like that of being comfortably filled with roast beef; love, like being enlivened with champagne."
Samuel Johnson, Scholar

The refrigerator light goes on...
This is the perfect accompaniment for roasts whether it's beef, chicken or lamb. A single pan, an oven, some herbs and you're good to go.

Nutrition Facts	
Serving size	about 2 Cups vegetables
Servings	4
Calories 215	Calories from Fat 35
	% Daily Value
Total Fat 4 g	6 %
Saturated Fat 1 g	3 %
Trans Fat 0 g	
Monounsaturated Fat 3 g	
Cholesterol 0 mg	0 %
Sodium 203 mg	8 %
Total Carbohydrates 43 g	15 %
Dietary Fiber 6 g	26 %
Sugars 6 g	
Protein 5 g	
Vitamin A 201 %	Vitamin C 45 %
Calcium 8 %	Iron 12 %
Vitamin K 25 mcg	
Potassium 1091 mg	
Magnesium 61 mg	

Sauteed Leeks

Servings = 2
Serving size = about 1 1/2 Cups

This recipe can easily be multiplied but does not make very good leftovers.

2 medium	leeks
	spray olive oil
1/8 tsp.	salt
to taste	fresh ground black pepper

Rinse the leeks well. Cut the stem end off and any dried leaf tips of the dark green tops.

Slice in half lengthwise. Rinse again to remove any dirt from the inside of the leeks. Slice the leeks cross-wise to separate the dark green tops from the white.

Slice both the tops and the bottom part of the leeks lengthwise into strips 1/4 inch to 1/2 inch wide. Keep the dark green tops and the bottom part of the leeks separate.

Spray a large skillet with olive oil and place the pan over medium-high heat. Add the dark green part of the leeks. Let the strips cook for about 5 minutes. Stir occasionally. They should brown only slightly.

After they have wilted somewhat, add the light green-white bottoms. Simply place them on top of the cooking dark green strips. Reduce the heat slightly. Let them cook for about two minutes and they will steam slightly, then begin to toss them to mix together with the dark green tops.

Add the salt and pepper. As you toss the leeks, adjust the heat to be hot enough to wilt the leeks and brown them only very lightly. They are done when the dark green tops are easily cut with a dinner knife -- about 20 minutes total cooking time.

"Persons living entirely on vegetables are seldom of a plump and succulent habit."
William Cullen, Physician

The refrigerator light goes on...
This is a deceptively simple recipe. Often the easiest and least complex dishes are. Leeks are so fantastic and cooking them like this where they slightly caramelize brings out the natural sweetness. This goes great as a side dish with almost any savory meal.

Nutrition Facts	
Serving size	about 1 1/2 Cups
Servings	2
Calories 88	Calories from Fat 23
	% Daily Value
Total Fat 3 g	4 %
Saturated Fat 0 g	0 %
Trans Fat 0 g	
Monounsaturated Fat 2 g	
Cholesterol 0 mg	0 %
Sodium 174 mg	7 %
Total Carbohydrates 16 g	5 %
Dietary Fiber 2 g	8 %
Sugars 4 g	
Protein 2 g	
Vitamin A 37 %	Vitamin C 22 %
Calcium 7 %	Iron 13 %
Vitamin K 54 mcg	
Potassium 202 mg	
Magnesium 31 mg	

Shredded Brussels Sprouts

Servings = 4
Serving size = 4 ounces Brussels sprouts

This recipe can easily be multiplied. I do like the left-overs chilled on sandwiches, but they're not so good by themselves.

1 lb.	Brussels sprouts
1 Tbsp.	maple syrup
1/8 tsp.	salt
2 Tbsp.	light spread (like Promise Buttery Spread Light or Smart Balance Light)

Purchase Brussels sprouts on the large side (about 2 inches wide).

Lay the Brussels sprout on its side. Slice across the sprout beginning at the top and working toward the stem. The slices should be about 2 – 3 mm thick. After all of the sprouts are sliced pick through them and remove the center of the sections that are the solid, tough stem. While doing this break the slices up into shredded segments.

Place the shredded sprouts in a steamer basket in a medium stock-pot with about an inch of water in the bottom of the pot.

Steam over high heat until slightly tender (about 7 - 10 minutes)

While steaming, place the maple syrup, salt and Promise in a medium mixing bowl.

Add the cooked Brussels sprouts to the bowl and toss until the sauce is melted and well blended. Serve immediately.

"We kids feared many things in those days - werewolves, dentists, North Koreans, Sunday School - but they all paled in comparison with Brussels sprouts."

Dave Barry, American humorist

The refrigerator light goes on...
Mr. Barry may be right about the Brussels Sprouts that he had as a kid, but these are amazing. The idea for shredding them is not mine but a friend's - Chef Michael Omo, from the Westin Lake Las Vegas. He served these to me at a lovely dinner in his home. At first I thought they were leeks, the flavor was so luscious and sweet. If you're like Dave Barry, try your Brussels sprouts a la Chef Omo.

Nutrition Facts	
Serving size	4 oz. Brussels sprouts
Servings	4
Calories 85	Calories from Fat 26
	% Daily Value
Total Fat 3 g	5 %
Saturated Fat 1 g	4 %
Trans Fat 0 g	
Monounsaturated Fat 1 g	
Cholesterol 0 mg	0 %
Sodium 143 mg	6 %
Total Carbohydrates 13 g	4 %
Dietary Fiber 4 g	17 %
Sugars 5 g	
Protein 4 g	
Vitamin A 24 %	Vitamin C 159 %
Calcium 5 %	Iron 9 %
Vitamin K 200 mcg	
Potassium 448 mg	
Magnesium 27 mg	

Thick Cut Yam Fries

Servings = 2
Serving size = about 1 1/2 Cups fries

This recipe can easily be multiplied but does not make very good leftovers.

2 small	yams (about 5 ounces each)
1/8 tsp.	salt
to taste	fresh ground black pepper
1/8 tsp.	dried thyme leaves
	spray olive oil

Place a large skillet in the oven and set the preheat to 325°F.

Scrub the yams well and then cut into wedges. It's easiest to cut them in half lengthwise and then quarters and then eighths.

When the oven is hot spray the pan lightly with oil. Add the yam wedges and sprinkle the salt, pepper and thyme over the top. Spray lightly with olive oil.

Return the pan to the oven and cook for about 25 minutes, tossing frequently.

Serve hot.

"If life were fair, Dan Quayle would be making a living asking, 'Do you want fries with that?'"
John Cleese, Genius

The refrigerator light goes on...
This recipe is so simple you just have to do it. The prep takes all of two minutes. Tossing them into a pan and watching them another two minutes. Great fries to go with that steak or burger in thirty minutes total. Easy!

Nutrition Facts	
Serving size	about 1 1/2 Cups fries
Servings	2
Calories 185	Calories from Fat 22
	% Daily Value
Total Fat 2 g	4 %
Saturated Fat 0 g	2 %
Trans Fat 0 g	
Monounsaturated Fat 2 g	
Cholesterol 0 mg	0 %
Sodium 164 mg	7 %
Total Carbohydrates 39 g	13 %
Dietary Fiber 6 g	23 %
Sugars 1 g	
Protein 2 g	
Vitamin A 4 %	Vitamin C 40 %
Calcium 3 %	Iron 5 %
Vitamin K 6 mcg	
Potassium 1143 mg	
Magnesium 30 mg	

Basque Chicken Stew

4 **120 min.**

Serving size = about 2 1/2 Cups

This recipe can easily be multiplied and makes great left-overs. Keeps well, refrigerated, for 2-3 days.

1/4 tsp.	saffron threads
1/2 Cup	boiling water
2 tsp.	olive oil
2 cloves	garlic (sliced)
1 large	onion (sliced into half moons)
1 lb.	boneless skinless chicken thighs (cubed)
2 tsp.	paprika
1/2 tsp.	salt
to taste	fresh ground black pepper
1 15-ounce can	no salt added diced tomatoes
4 Cups	water
1 Cup	lentils
1 medium	green bell pepper (julienned)
1 medium	yellow bell pepper (julienned)

Place the saffron in a small cup. Pour the boiling water over the threads and let stand for at least 20 minutes.

Preheat the oven to 325°F.

Place the olive oil in a large ovenproof pot (Dutch oven is best) over medium heat. Add the garlic and cook for about 2 minutes stirring frequently.

Add the onions and cook for about 5 minutes stirring frequently until they are slightly soft.

Add the chicken and cook stirring frequently for 3 minutes until lightly browned.

Add the paprika, salt, pepper, tomatoes, water, lentils and peppers. Stir well.

Add the saffron water with the saffron threads and stir.

Cover and place in the oven. Cook for about 90 minutes to 2 hours. Stir about every 20 minutes.

Serve.

"A little bad taste is like a splash of paprika. We all need a splash of bad taste. It's hearty, it's healthy, it's physical."

Diana Vreeland, Fashion editor

The refrigerator light goes on...
The warmth of saffron and paprika together is really magical. The savory, aromatic flavor of the saffron with the spicy smokiness of the paprika are perfect with the chicken and lentils. This recipe takes about 15 minutes to prep and get into the oven and the wait for the stew to be done is oh, so worth it.

Nutrition Facts	
Serving size	about 2 1/2 Cups
Servings	4
Calories 420	Calories from Fat 64
	% Daily Value
Total Fat 8 g	13 %
Saturated Fat 1 g	5 %
Trans Fat 0 g	
Monounsaturated Fat 2 g	
Cholesterol 96 mg	32 %
Sodium 410 mg	17 %
Total Carbohydrates 53 g	18 %
Dietary Fiber 17 g	68 %
Sugars 9 g	
Protein 39 g	
Vitamin A 18 %	Vitamin C 211 %
Calcium 12 %	Iron 40 %
Vitamin K 17 mcg	
Potassium 1305 mg	
Magnesium 123 mg	

Broccoli Cheese Soup

6 **60 min.**

Serving size = about 12 ounces as an entree

This recipe can easily be multiplied and keeps well for 3-4 days in the refrigerator. Reheat gently.

Serve with a 2 ounce whole grain roll and a side salad of your choice.

2 lbs.	broccoli
4 Cups	water
2 tsp.	extra virgin olive oil
1/2 medium	white onion (diced)
4 Tbsp.	all purpose white flour
2 Cups	1% milk
1/2 tsp.	salt
8 ounces	reduced-fat cheddar cheese (shredded)

Cut the crowns from the stems of the broccoli. Divide the crowns into small flowerets and set aside.

Using a potato peeler, peel the stems to expose the tender center. Dice the peeled stems. Place them in a stock pot with the four cups of water on medium-high and boil until tender. This will take about 30 minutes and the water will be reduced by about half.

While the stems are boiling, steam the flowerets until they are bright green and slightly tender. After they are cool, chop finely.

After the stems are soft, puree them until smooth using a blender or stick blender.

Place the olive oil in a medium stock-pot over medium-high heat and add the onions. Reduce the heat to medium and cook slowly until soft. Add the flour and stir until well blended. Add the milk and stir. Add the pureed broccoli stems and half of the chopped broccoli flowerets and salt.

As the soup thickens, blend it again using a blender or stick blender.

Add the remaining finely chopped broccoli flowerets and stir. As the soup reheats, add the cheese in 3 batches and allow it to melt.

Heat gently on low for about 15 minutes and serve.

"I live on good soup, not on fine words."
Moliere, Author

The refrigerator light goes on...
Soup nights are the best. In the winter, a hearty soup like this with a salad is all you need to fill up and be warm. A cool Gazpacho or fruit soup in the summer is the perfect way to chill out.

Nutrition Facts	
Serving size	12 ounces
Servings	6
Calories 193	Calories from Fat 50
	% Daily Value
Total Fat 6 g	9 %
Saturated Fat 3 g	13 %
Trans Fat 0 g	
Monounsaturated Fat 2 g	
Cholesterol 11 mg	4 %
Sodium 525 mg	22 %
Total Carbohydrates 20 g	7 %
Dietary Fiber 4 g	17 %
Sugars 3 g	
Protein 17 g	
Vitamin A 24 %	Vitamin C 229 %
Calcium 35 %	Iron 9 %
Vitamin K 156 mcg	
Potassium 672 mg	
Magnesium 53 mg	

Cannellini Bean Soup

 30 min.

Serving size = about 1 1/2 Cups

This recipe can easily be multiplied or halved. This recipe is also good chilled and will keep well in the refrigerator for about 72 hours.

Note: This recipe is labeled 30 minutes if you use canned beans. Using dried beans will increase the time required to 90 minutes after you soak the dried beans overnight.

Serve with a 2-ounce whole grain roll.

2 1/3 Cups	cannellini beans (or 2 15-ounce cans no salt added cannellini beans)
3 quarts	water
1 tsp.	olive oil
2 cloves	garlic (minced)
1 large	white onion (diced)
2 Cups	low sodium chicken or vegetable broth
1/4 tsp.	salt
2	ribs celery with leaves (minced)
2 Tbsp.	fresh oregano
to taste	fresh ground black pepper

Place the beans in a large pot and cover with water. Let the beans soak overnight. Drain the beans the next day and cover with water, then place over medium-high heat. Bring to a boil and reduce the heat to a simmer. Let the beans cook for about an hour until soft.

Drain the beans and set aside. Rinse the pot well. (Alternatively use 2 - 15 ounce cans no salt added cannellini beans.)

Place the olive oil in the same pot over medium heat. Add the garlic and white onion. Cook slowly over medium until the onions are translucent. Add the beans back to the pot and stir well.

Add the chicken stock and salt. Cook for about 10 minutes stirring occasionally. Add the celery, fresh oregano and black pepper. Cook for about 20 minutes.

Using a stick blender (or a conventional blender in batches), blend the soup until it is pureed. The soup may be served hot or chilled.

"Soup puts the heart at ease, calms down the violence of hunger, eliminates the tension of the day, and awakens and refines the appetite."
Auguste Escoffier, Chef

The refrigerator light goes on...
This is an easy soup to make. It takes a little time to cook, but the hardest part is chopping the onions and celery. Thick and creamy, it makes a great summer dinner with a salad and a whole wheat roll.

Nutrition Facts	
Serving size	about 1 1/2 Cups
Servings	4
Calories 225	Calories from Fat 21
	% Daily Value
Total Fat 2 g	4 %
Saturated Fat 1 g	3 %
Trans Fat 0 g	
Monounsaturated Fat 1 g	
Cholesterol 0 mg	0 %
Sodium 207 mg	9 %
Total Carbohydrates 39 g	13 %
Dietary Fiber 9 g	34 %
Sugars 3 g	
Protein 14 g	
Vitamin A 33 %	Vitamin C 7 %
Calcium 14 %	Iron 29 %
Vitamin K 14 mcg	
Potassium 917 mg	
Magnesium 87 mg	

Corn Chowder

 90 min.

Serving size = about 1 1/2 Cups

This recipe can easily be multiplied by 2. This soup is better if it cools and sits in the fridge overnight. Keeps well for about 48 to 72 hours.

Seve with a 2-ounce whole wheat roll.

2 Tbsp.	unsalted butter
2 Cups	white onion (diced)
4 cloves	garlic (minced)
2 lbs.	russet potatoes (peeled and cubed)
4	ears corn kernels (3 cups)
2 Cups	low sodium chicken or vegetable broth
3 Cups	2% milk
1 tsp.	fresh thyme leaves
1/4 tsp.	salt
1/8 tsp.	pepper

Melt butter in a medium stock pot over medium low heat.

Add the minced garlic and onion and cook very gently. Stir frequently and do not allow to brown. After about ten minutes the onions will be translucent and slightly soft. Add the potatoes, corn, chicken stock and milk.

Simmer over very low heat for about an hour. Do not allow the soup to boil.

Add the fresh thyme, salt and pepper and cook for fifteen minutes longer.

Remove and allow to cool and then chill at least overnight.

Reheat soup very gently for about 20 minutes before serving.

"Sex is good, but not as good as fresh sweet corn."
Garrison Keillor, Humorist

The refrigerator light goes on...
The difference between this and my Clam Chowder recipe (at www.DrGourmet.com) is the choice of potato. The waxy red potatoes will not thicken a soup as well as the more fragile russets, which will break down slowly to make the soup creamy.

Nutrition Facts	
Serving size	about 1 1/2 Cups
Servings	6
Calories 313	Calories from Fat 65
	% Daily Value
Total Fat 7 g	11 %
Saturated Fat 4 g	21 %
Trans Fat 0 g	
Monounsaturated Fat 2 g	
Cholesterol 21 mg	7 %
Sodium 520 mg	22 %
Total Carbohydrates 54 g	18 %
Dietary Fiber 6 g	26 %
Sugars 13 g	
Protein 12 g	
Vitamin A 6 %	Vitamin C 69 %
Calcium 22 %	Iron 11 %
Vitamin K 4 mcg	
Potassium 1184 mg	
Magnesium 90 mg	

Cream of Potato Soup with Roasted Garlic

4 **30 min.**

Serving size = about 2 Cups

This recipe can easily be multiplied and makes great leftovers.

This recipe requires making Roasted Garlic (recipe included).

Serve with Cole Slaw or Zucchini Salad (recipes included).

1 tsp.	olive oil
1 small	white onion (diced)
12 ounces	Idaho potato (peeled and cubed)
4 Cups	water
1 Cup	2% milk
1	bulb roasted garlic
1/4 tsp.	salt
to taste	fresh ground black pepper
12 ounces	Yukon Gold potato (peeled and cubed)
4 ounces	smoked gouda cheese (shredded)

Place the olive oil in a medium sauce pan over medium heat. Add the onion and cook for about 4 minutes, stirring frequently. Do not allow the onion to brown.

Add the Idaho potato and water. Reduce the heat to medium and simmer for about 30 minutes until the potatoes are soft.

Add the milk, roasted garlic, salt and pepper. Using a blender or stick blender puree until smooth.

Return the soup to medium heat and add the Yukon gold potatoes. Cook for about 20 minutes until the potatoes are soft.

Serve each bowl of soup topped with one ounce of smoked gouda.

"You can never have enough garlic. With enough garlic, you can eat The New York Times."
Morley Safer, Journalist

The refrigerator light goes on...
On a cold fall or winter night there's nothing more comforting than a bowl of potato soup. This recipe is so savory with the garlic and smoked gouda and makes the perfect meal with a simple side salad.

Nutrition Facts	
Serving size	about 2 Cups
Servings	4
Calories 322	Calories from Fat 100
	% Daily Value
Total Fat 11 g	18 %
Saturated Fat 6 g	30 %
Trans Fat 0 g	
Monounsaturated Fat 4 g	
Cholesterol 37 mg	12 %
Sodium 422 mg	18 %
Total Carbohydrates 43 g	14 %
Dietary Fiber 4 g	14 %
Sugars 6 g	
Protein 13 g	
Vitamin A 3 %	Vitamin C 30 %
Calcium 32 %	Iron 5 %
Vitamin K 6 mcg	
Potassium 768 mg	
Magnesium 56 mg	

Lentil Chili

4 **75 min.**

Serving size = about 2 Cups

This recipe can easily be multiplied and makes great leftovers.

1 Tbsp.	olive oil
2 cloves	garlic (sliced)
1 large	onion (diced)
1 15-ounce can	no salt added crushed tomatoes
1 Tbsp.	chili powder
2 tsp.	ground cumin
1 tsp.	dried oregano
1/2	chipotle pepper in adobo sauce (optional) (minced)
to taste	fresh ground black pepper
5 Cups	water
1 Cup	lentils
6 Tbsp.	non-fat sour cream
3 ounces	reduced-fat Monterey jack cheese (shredded)

Place the olive oil in a large saucepan, over medium heat.

Add the garlic and onion and cook, stirring frequently, until the onions have softened.

Add the crushed tomatoes, chili powder, cumin, oregano, chipotle (if used) and pepper, and stir well.

Add the five cups of water and the lentils, and stir well.

Reduce heat to medium-low and simmer until lentils are cooked through but not mushy, approximately 45 minutes to an hour.

Serve with 1 tablespoon sour cream and 1/2 ounce Monterey jack cheese per serving.

"Rain or Snow,
To Chili go,
You'll find it so,
For ought we know.
Time will show."

Benjamin Franklin, Statesman

The refrigerator light goes on...
This is a fine chili that's a snap to make, full of flavor and really great for you. It has it all: low calorie, low fat, high fiber, garlic, cheese, sour cream – all the great things in life. It's not too spicy and those with GERD should be fine if they leave out the chipotle pepper since there's not much cumin or chili powder in each serving.

Nutrition Facts		
Serving size		about 2 Cups
Servings		4
Calories 421	Calories from Fat 127	
		% Daily Value
Total Fat 14 g		22 %
Saturated Fat 7 g		34 %
Trans Fat 0 g		
Monounsaturated Fat 5 g		
Cholesterol 29 mg		10 %
Sodium 419 mg		17 %
Total Carbohydrates 48 g		16 %
Dietary Fiber 19 g		74 %
Sugars 5 g		
Protein 28 g		
Vitamin A 35 %	Vitamin C 32 %	
Calcium 43 %	Iron 36 %	
Vitamin K 9 mcg		
Potassium 1001 mg		
Magnesium 105 mg		

Pasta Fagioli with Chicken

 60 min.

Serving size = about 2 1/2 Cups

This recipe can easily be multiplied, makes great leftovers, and freezes well.

3 tsp.	olive oil
8 ounces	boneless skinless chicken thighs (diced)
4 cloves	garlic (minced)
1 large	onion (diced)
3 large	ribs celery (diced)
2 15-ounce cans	no salt added diced tomatoes
1/2 tsp.	salt
to taste	fresh ground black pepper
2 tsp.	dried basil
2 tsp.	dried oregano
1/2 tsp.	dried red pepper flakes
6 Cups	water
8 ounces	whole wheat pasta (spirals or shells)
2 15-ounce cans	no salt added navy beans (drained and rinsed)
3 ounces	Parmigiano-Reggiano (grated)

Place 2 teaspoons of the olive oil in a large stock pot over medium heat.

Add the chicken and cook for about 5 minutes or until browned. Remove to a plate.

Add the remaining teaspoon of olive oil to the pot.

Add the garlic and cook, stirring frequently, for about 3 minutes. Do not let the garlic brown.

Add the onion and celery and cook for about 3 minutes, stirring frequently.

Add the tomatoes, salt, pepper, basil, oregano, red pepper flakes, water and stir. Simmer for about 30 minutes.

Add the pasta and beans and cook for about 20 minutes, stirring occasionally.

Add the grated parmesan, stir well and serve.

"Soup is a lot like a family. Each ingredient enhances the others; each batch has its own characteristics; and it needs time to simmer to reach full flavor."

Marge Kennedy, Author

The refrigerator light goes on...
There are hundreds of variations of this soup. The basics are tomatoes, some pasta and beans. Herbs run the gamut and include sage, basil, oregano and rosemary.

This is the perfect cold weather soup that has it all – veggies, legumes, lean flavorful chicken, whole grain pasta and great Italian flavors. I created this variation with the chicken to make this dish a complete meal.

The recipe takes all of about 20 minutes prep time and making a double or triple batch ensures that you have a lot on hand for leftovers during the week.

Nutrition Facts	
Serving size	about 2 1/2 Cups
Servings	6
Calories 428	Calories from Fat 77
	% Daily Value
Total Fat 9 g	15 %
Saturated Fat 2 g	13 %
Trans Fat 0 g	
Monounsaturated Fat 3 g	
Cholesterol 41 mg	14 %
Sodium 487 mg	21 %
Total Carbohydrates 63 g	21 %
Dietary Fiber 15 g	52 %
Sugars 5 g	
Protein 26 g	
Vitamin A 7 %	Vitamin C 29 %
Calcium 33 %	Iron 34 %
Vitamin K 18 mcg	
Potassium 905 mg	
Magnesium 140 mg	

Quick Chicken Noodle Soup

 30 min.

Serving size = about 2 Cups

This recipe can easily be multiplied and makes great leftovers.

2 tsp.	olive oil
1 lb.	boneless skinless chicken thighs (cut into 1 inch cubes)
1 medium	onion (diced)
3	ribs celery (sliced)
3 medium	carrots (peeled and sliced)
2 Cups	low sodium chicken broth
1/4 tsp.	salt
to taste	fresh ground black pepper
1/2 tsp.	dried tarragon
4 quarts	water (divided)
6 ounces	egg noodles
2 Tbsp.	fresh parsley (coarsely chopped)

Place 1 teaspoon of olive oil in a large sauce pan over medium high heat.

When the oil is hot add the cubed chicken and cook, stirring frequently, until lightly browned. Remove to a plate.

Add 1 teaspoon olive oil and then the diced onion. Cook, stirring frequently, for about 4 – 5 minutes. Add the celery and cook for another 3 minutes.

Add the chicken, carrots, chicken stock, salt, pepper, tarragon and 4 cups of water.

Reduce the heat and let simmer for 45 minutes. Stir occasionally.

Place the remaining 3 quarts water in a large stock pot over high heat. When boiling add the noodles. Boil for about 10 minutes until just tender.

Drain the noodles and place in the bottom of serving bowls. Add the parsley and then top with the soup. Serve.

"Next to hot chicken soup, a tattoo of an anchor on your chest, and penicillin, I consider a honeymoon one of the most overrated events in the world."
Erma Bombeck, Housewife

The refrigerator light goes on...
(Almost) everybody loves Chicken Noodle Soup. There's just not a much better meal and if you are getting yours from a can, this is the easy compromise. It does take a little longer than opening a can, but the reward is so great! This recipe is all of about 10 minutes active cooking time and it's oh, so worth it with true chicken flavor.

Cooking the noodles separately is key. It allows you to keep the soup from becoming cloudy with the starch from the noodles and to precisely cook them 'til they are just done. Add them to the soup with the fresh parsley at the last minute for that fresh, fresh flavor.

Nutrition Facts	
Serving size	about 2 Cups
Servings	4
Calories 368	Calories from Fat 73
	% Daily Value
Total Fat 8 g	13 %
Saturated Fat 2 g	9 %
Trans Fat 0 g	
Monounsaturated Fat 3 g	
Cholesterol 93 mg	31 %
Sodium 338 mg	14 %
Total Carbohydrates 42 g	14 %
Dietary Fiber 4 g	15 %
Sugars 6 g	
Protein 31 g	
Vitamin A 160 %	Vitamin C 15 %
Calcium 6 %	Iron 18 %
Vitamin K 50 mcg	
Potassium 749 mg	
Magnesium 64 mg	

93004982R00079

Made in the USA
Lexington, KY
11 July 2018